The Care & Feeding of Trees

The Care & Feeding of Trees

NEW, UPDATED EDITION

Richard C. Murphy
William E. Meyer

ILLUSTRATED BY
CLARA MAY HANKINS

CROWN PUBLISHERS, INC., NEW YORK

*To the millions of homeowners
who share with us a true love and appreciation
for trees*

Published by Crown Publishers, Inc., One Park Avenue, New York, New York 10016, and simultaneously in Canada by General Publishing Company Limited

Manufactured in the United States of America

Library of Congress Cataloging in Publication Data
Murphy, Richard C., 1930–
  The care and feeding of trees.

  Bibliography: p.
  Includes index.
  1. Trees, care of. 2. Tree planting. I. Meyer,
William E., 1923– . II. Title.
SB435.M84 1983 635.9'77 82-23491
ISBN: 0-517-548917

10 9 8 7 6 5 4 3 2 1
First Updated Edition

ACKNOWLEDGMENTS

For their kind and thoughtful assistance in our research efforts, we wish to thank the following persons: Professor Ralph G. Unger of the State University College of Forestry at Syracuse University; Professor Lawrence S. Hamilton of the New York State College of Agriculture at Cornell University; Professor J. G. Matthysse of the New York State College of Agriculture at Cornell University; Dr. P. W. Oman, formerly of the insect identification and parasite introduction laboratories of the United States Department of Agriculture; Walter Androsko, Westchester County, New York, Agricultural Agent, United States Department of Agriculture; and Robert L. Rudd of the Department of Zoology, University of California.

PREFACE

Though tree care is just as important as gardening, much less is generally known about it. Thousands of homeowners sadly neglect the important trees around their homes; as a result, the trees suffer from malnutrition, thirst, sunscald, fungi infections, insect attacks, and a host of other evils.

The purpose of our book is quite simple: We want to give easy-to-understand information about the care and raising of trees to all those people who want shade, comfort, beauty, and safety, as well as the luxury of fruits and nuts growing on their grounds. This book will enable the layman to know more about his trees, have a greater appreciation and understanding of them, and it will help him to perform routine tree-care chores himself—from planting to pruning—thus saving time and money, as well as his favorite trees. It will be useful as a reference or handbook, and can be used as a guide in calendaring tree chores during the entire year.

Hopefully, this book will also lead to a greater love of trees and to a fuller appreciation of the magnificent contribution they make to our lives.

RICHARD C. MURPHY
WILLIAM E. MEYER

CONTENTS

Make Safety a Part of Your Plans

"It won't happen to me!"

Too many people think so—until they suffer an accident when least prepared.

Tree work is dangerous. It is not like tinkering around the garden. Booby traps lurk everywhere— weak limbs, a defective ladder, a hidden hole, poison ivy, and various other hazards. But tree work can be safe.

To help you prepare for your backyard job, we have listed some special safety tips at the conclusions of five of our eight chapters. Be safety-conscious whenever you do your tree work. It will pay off.

TREES AND TREE CARE

The Value of Trees

❧ HOW A TREELESS WORLD WOULD AFFECT US. Have you ever stopped to think just how truly wonderful a tree is? Or are you one of those who take trees for granted?

If we were to lose every tree, the consequences would be worse than those of any depression or war, making life far more difficult than ever before—that is, for as long as life continued.

The first effects of a treeless world probably would take place in our rivers and streams. First they would become muddy as the result of soil erosion, which is normally controlled by the roots of trees holding earth in place. Then the dirt carried by the rivers eventually would be deposited in the beds of important harbors and in shipping lanes.

Take the Hudson River in New York, for example. Without forests upriver in the mountainous areas, the Hudson—with New York City at its mouth—would become so shallow that one of the busiest thoroughfares of shipping and commerce would be irreparably damaged. As important as it is, New York City's harbor would have to be closed to the many large vessels it serves, since it would be virtually impossible to keep such waterways dredged.

Without trees, electric power—so vital to our homes, hospitals, and industries—would also be affected. The formation of new tributaries along eroded riverbanks would cut down on the speed of flow so necessary to turn the turbines that still furnish much of this country's electric power. In fact, erosion control is an ever-present problem, and electric power companies have been taking remedial steps by planting trees around the areas of waterfalls and rapids.

In the springtime, an absence of trees would mean floods. In the summertime most rivers—probably all—would dry up because of the intense heat from the sun. Flash floods resulting from heavy rainfall would occur. Places normally shielded by forests would suffer the most because they would no longer have protection from cold or hot winds. Examples of such conditions resulting from deforestation actually occurred early this century in many parts of Asia and Europe, and even in this country (in Pennsylvania), where entire forests were cut down for their lumber.

A treeless world would also affect available drinking water. Watershed areas would no longer have a protective covering from the sun, and the spongy forest floor, which ordinarily aids in the storage of water supplies, would dry up. As a result, it would be just a matter of time before reservoirs—and streams from the hilly, wooded areas that feed them—were drained through usage and evaporation. Eventually, gusts of wind would blow away large amounts of dried-up soil, and torrential floods would complete the damage.

All this could add up to only one climax: the birth of one great desert and the possible extinction of life. This may be the story behind the formation of the Sahara and other deserts. Evidence that the Sahara Desert was comparatively fertile and well populated until about four thousand years ago was revealed in recent years, according to an article, "The Painted Caves of the Tassili," by Robert Littell in *Reader's Digest*, September, 1958. In 1963, Karl Oedekoven, Near East regional forestry officer for the Food and Agriculture Organization of the United Nations, wrote in *Unasylva*, the FAO's international review of forestry and forest products, that as late as A.D. 1497, permanent villages were recorded in areas of the Sahara Desert where there is now nothing but sand. According to an article, "Reforestation Gains in Spain," published in *The Christian Science Monitor* of September 24, 1963, reforestation in some areas of Spain is credited with changing weather patterns that have caused a substantial increase in rainfall. And according to the Michelin Guide *Gorges du Tarn: Cévennes, Bas Languedoc* for 1966–1967, in the Cévennes Mountains of France, between 1875 and 1962, under the direction of Georges Fabre and his successors, more than 33,000 acres of denuded mountain slopes were reforested in the region of Mount Aigoual, avoiding a recurrence of the disastrous floods, sometimes with crests of water sixty feet high, that devastated the valleys of the Tarn at the beginning of the century.

ॐ OTHER BENEFITS OF TREES. Trees are quite important as homes for our friends the birds. Without birds, the great protection they give to plant life by feeding on harmful, destructive insects would be missing. Without vegetation, on which animals depend for their food, our meat supplies would disappear.

Trees are also important as a source of many foods and supplies that fill our everyday needs. From trees come fruits, nuts, syrups, sugar, edible leaves, and roots; timber for building homes; wood for furniture, pencils, and charcoal; paper for the daily newspaper you buy; rubber to manufacture tires, galoshes, and garden hose; turpentine for your home-painting projects; and scores of other products we take for granted.

The Abilities of a Tree

&▶ TREES ARE LIVING, BREATHING CREATURES. The fact that trees are, in many ways, like intelligent beings may come as somewhat of a surprise to you. This can be explained clearly as follows:

1. *A tree eats.* Its tiny hairlike roots beneath the earth's surface are always on the hunt for such elements in the soil as nitrogen, calcium, phosphorus, potassium, iron, copper, zinc, and magnesium.

2. *A tree drinks.* A generous supply of water is required for carrying nutrients from the soil through the "digestive system" of the tree.

3. *A tree digests its food.* A tree has a digestive tract. Like a plumbing system, it functions as elements from the soil flow through microscopic ducts in the sapwood from the tiniest of root hairs to the most distant of leaves where tree food is formed on contact with sunlight and CO_2. The food is then carried through the tree to build up layers of cells in the cambium (the inner skin or growing tissue). Tree growth and root development result. (See Figure 1.)

4. *A tree breathes.* Like all living matter, a tree requires air. A hard, packed soil in the root zone of the tree will cut off the tree's breathing. Supplies of oxygen and carbon dioxide vital to the manufacture of food are absorbed through the soil by the roots, as well as from the atmosphere by the leaves.

5. *A tree reproduces.* The tree is capable of rearing its own family. Many seeds have wings that, with an assist by winds, carry them to points away from the parent tree. There, soil and sunlight sufficiently permit new, fast growth.

6. *A tree "talks."* Listen to trees the next time the leaves rustle in

the wind. Thomas Hardy confirmed this when he wrote, "At the passing of a breeze the fir trees sob and moan—the ash hisses—the beech rustles."

7. *A tree sleeps.* In the winter months, when deciduous trees lose their leaves and the growing processes of evergreens slow down, a tree is getting its rest.

8. *A tree has healing powers.* A scar, if properly treated, will usually heal as long as the tree is alive and growing.

But many mysteries about trees still remain for science to solve. Whether a tree actually "thinks," for example, is questionable. There has been some evidence indicating it may, and this has been revealed in studies of root growth. Some roots, it has been shown, will stop and return toward the tree when they encounter a rock or other object. Others will bypass a rock by going around it. There are even some that head for the slightest crack in a rock, splitting it as they continue their search for food.

Just as there is still much to learn about the human body and the human mind, there is still a great deal we do not know about trees: Does a tree have willpower? Does it have a nervous system? Does it possess powers of locomotion? What causes certain diseases, such as Dutch elm disease, and how can they be prevented and remedied? These are just a few of the many questions that someday may be answered.

❧ THE TREE KEEPS ITS OWN DIARY. If you've ever kept a diary, you know how interesting it is to look back to incidents of the past. If you have a very large tree on your property, that tree probably has a story at least as interesting to tell. And while it doesn't come out with such details as how your grandfather proposed to your grandmother at that very spot, it does reveal some startling facts.

For instance, that tree can tell you when there were trees in its vicinity and on which side of it they were located. You can determine approximately what years there were unusual summer seasons and approximately when it was attacked by disease. It can also tell little tales associated with man-made objects found inside it.

Most of this information is recorded in circular-shaped growths—one for each year—in the trunk cross section or core of the tree. (See Figure 1.) These rings, as they are called, are usually visible only after a tree is cut down. However, professional tree men have devised methods of boring through the tree trunk, without disastrous effects to a living tree, to remove a section clearly outlining the seasonal growths. Such a section would be as long in length as the diameter of the tree trunk.

Figure 1

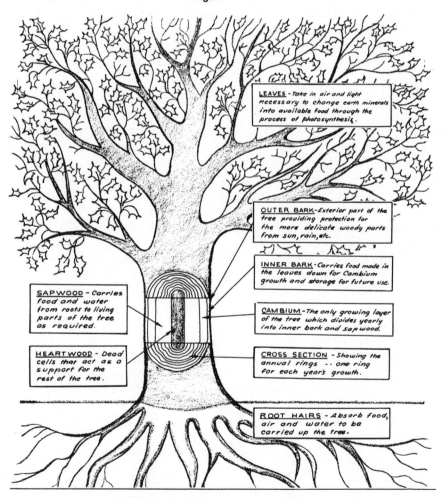

LEAVES - Take in air and light necessary to change earth minerals into available food through the process of photosynthesis.

OUTER BARK - Exterior part of the tree providing protection for the more delicate woody parts from sun, rain, etc.

INNER BARK - Carries food made in the leaves down for Cambium growth and storage for future use.

SAPWOOD - Carries food and water from roots to living parts of the tree as required.

CAMBIUM - The only growing layer of the tree which divides yearly into inner bark and sapwood.

HEARTWOOD - Dead cells that act as a support for the rest of the tree.

CROSS SECTION - Showing the annual rings -- one ring for each year's growth.

ROOT HAIRS - Absorb food, air and water to be carried up the tree.

THE COMPONENTS OF A TREE

A large dead elm tree on the property of one of the authors had a story all its own. The tree was more than one hundred years old, dating from Abraham Lincoln's time. There were also symptoms indicating that the tree suffered an attack of Dutch elm disease in the 1930's but managed to survive. (A little research later uncovered old government-issued documents verifying a Dutch elm disease epidemic at that time.) Finally, a short piece of barbed wire embedded inches inside the tree trunk was discovered; it was part of a barbed-wire fence that once had been erected next to the tree. (It was learned that the grounds had been occupied by a pig farm.)

The Need for Looking After Trees

ॐ CARE OF YOUR TREES MAKES SENSE. Some people argue that trees can take care of themselves. Of course they do—but only to a certain degree. They seek and find their own food and water. They have the sturdiness to buck the strongest of winds and unusually miserable weather—most of the time. They are endowed with healing powers, and even overcome disease at times.

Naturally, a tree survives best in the forest or in a wooded area. On the forest floor layers of rotted leaves help fertilize the soil. In the summertime, the overhead umbrella of leaves prevents rapid evaporation of water that saturates the ground. What better conditions could there be to afford trees a good, long-lasting supply of food and water?

Insects—considered the worst enemies of trees—do not seem to have the damaging effect on trees in a forest or wooded area that they do when a tree is in the open. This is probably because there are greater numbers of trees from which the insects can choose, and any one tree is not apt to be singled out and affected; also, there are greater numbers of birds to feed on the insects.

But this doesn't mean that trees in the woods will outlive the trees that you plant and care for on your premises. Forest trees do die from various causes. During storms, for example, they may topple because the soft, spongy ground is not fully capable of supporting their weight. This is particularly true of the top-heavy trees that grew taller to reach the sunlight high above the foliage of the thick forest.

Furthermore, decay is common in the forest. Branches die and fall off, leaving slight indentations where they once projected from the trunk. These collect rainwater, and, in time, decay forms and eats its way inwardly, later causing the tree to collapse because of insufficient trunk support.

ह•» MAN'S CARELESSNESS: A THREAT TO TREES. Trees that may have taken as many as fifty or more years to grow in the forest may be irreparably damaged in just a few days. All it takes is several moments of carelessness. Usually, disaster to trees occurs when an area is undergoing development or redevelopment. The roots of trees may be indiscriminately severed in digging operations. The penetration of moisture and air around the base and root zones of trees may be obstructed by sidewalks, driveways, and tamped-down soil caused by the traffic of heavy construction equipment. Then, too, trees are deprived of food when leaves are removed from lawn areas. Damage may be inflicted in the form of bark scrapes, and other injuries may be caused by fire, smoke, and chemicals.

ह•» COST OF CARE VS. COST OF "REPAIR." A new homeowner knew it was going to cost money when he requested professional advice from a tree expert. But how much? Buying a new home had been financially burdensome, and now he was faced with a decision on whether to spend more money. At the time, there were some fifty trees crowded on his property. Many of them had been buried in fill (during grading operations) as much as four or five feet deep. The builder—either careless or unaware that such fill endangers trees—graded to meet whatever requirements were placed upon him. Since practically every tree bore scars of the "battle of the bulldozer," they were exposed to a full-scale attack by insects and disease. The foliage of the trees appeared thin; every leaf looked like lace.

One of the tree expert's suggestions was to feed the trees as soon as possible. He also advised the removal of as much dirt as could be conveniently taken away from the base of every tree. The estimated costs sounded expensive. But, in reasoning out the problem, it appeared to be worth getting a bit more in debt at that time than spending hundreds of dollars later just to cut down and cart away a group of dead trees.

The feeding of the trees and the excavation of the excess fill at their bases saved the trees. Five years later, not a single tree that had been given the proper care was lost. Such good results are attributed to early care. This was proved later when trees elsewhere in the neighborhood died, largely because of neglect.

ও⚮ OTHER NECESSARY CARE. However, care of trees does not end with feeding and permitting them to breathe. Insects and disease, the danger of falling dead branches, and the appearance of the trees must also be considered. There are methods of controlling the harmful insects that eat tree foliage and the cambium, thereby endangering the life of the tree. And there are principles to follow for the safe, proper removal of dead branches.

A tree can live to a ripe old age, especially if it is helped a bit. All over the country there are examples of trees that have lasted for lengthy periods, including sycamores, oaks, elms, birches, maples, pines, spruces, yews, pecans, tulips, and cherries. These have been able to survive mainly because of their resistance to the many hazards that no doubt confronted them.[1] With the help of man, most of our trees can be helped and saved—but only through regular care. The late Richard R. Fenska, a prominent tree specialist for many years, and author of books written for professional tree experts, said, "Trees growing under favorable conditions, and not subject to injury or disease, will grow to a very old age."[2]

If you are moving into a new home, initial tree care—even with new plantings—may seem like a task. But a regular system—such as inspecting often and feeding as needed—will make this necessary work around the home easier. These and other hints for good tree care, along with economical do-it-yourself suggestions, are more fully explained later.

The home and tree owner who acquaints himself with the content of this volume, and then follows its precepts, will be amply rewarded. The dividends for his tree-growing efforts will be a comfortable home, beauty, privacy, food if he's interested in fruit and nut trees—and increased property value that will grow with the height of his trees.

[1] Dr. Ferdinand C. Lane, *The Story of Trees* (Doubleday & Co., Inc., Garden City, N.Y., 1952), p. 7.
[2] Richard R. Fenska, *Tree Experts Manual* (A. T. De La Mare Co., Inc., New York, 1947), p. 73.

2 PLANNING AND PLANTING

The Key to a Complete Home: Plenty of Trees

ॐ BE A GOOD PLANNER, PLANT NOW! Nothing else that nature provides for us in the vegetable world can mean as much as trees around our homes. They lend beauty to their setting, and enable us to reap many benefits for more enjoyable living. Plant all the flowers and shrubs you want, but their aroma, color, and beauty will never equal all a tree will give. Nor should you feel that your place is too small; no residential property is so restricted that it cannot accommodate at least one growing tree.

Be tree-conscious! Those who plant now are wise planners who, years from now, will be proud of their efforts, and future generations will be indebted to us.

One of the authors recalls that, as a child, he planted a three- or four-foot willow tree "whip" in front of his home. Today that tree towers high above the two-story house. Although many schools and municipal organizations observe Arbor Day with tree-planting programs, it would be interesting and constructive if *every* American youngster traditionally planted at least one tree annually and afterward was responsible for its care. Then he could proudly boast in later years, "This is *my* tree."

ॐ WHAT TREES MEAN TO THE HOMEOWNER. Trees add charm, beauty, color, interest, and an air of welcome. A house without trees around it looks incomplete and uninviting. But when, right in your own yard, you are able to witness nature's annual breathtaking performance—from the bursting of buds in the spring to her autumnal magnificence—it is a spectacular display.

Besides beauty, trees also give comfort. They provide relief from the direct rays of the sun, and help keep your home cool in the summertime. In winter, groups and groves of small trees serve as windbreaks, cutting heat bills and protecting your home against wind damage.

Trees allow privacy, too, because groupings of various kinds help to screen objectionable views. What better way is there of obtaining the privacy you may want for your backyard picnic nook or patio?

Figure 2

What trees do for the home.

The air around your home is purer and healthier, too, when there is an abundance of trees growing there. This is of particular importance when automobile traffic nearby is heavy. Human beings require oxygen, and most trees need carbon dioxide; trees counteract the carbon from engine exhausts with the oxygen they give off.

Trees make your grounds more inviting to birds, who always look for food and cover; and as a result, when you have trees in your yard, the nearby insect population is under constant attack.

Fruit and nut trees, along with the benefits of shade, privacy, and a healthful environment, of course provide delicious food.

Best of all, perhaps, trees help determine the value of your property—a value that literally grows as the trees grow. You'll get more for your property when you're ready to sell.

But trees *do* take time to mature, so you should start planning for the future *now*.

How to Establish a Tree Plan for Your Property

ह&ल THE FIRST STEP IN TREE LANDSCAPING: TAKE INVENTORY. Whether you are doing your own tree landscaping or having it done professionally, it is important that you know something about what's involved.

Let us suppose your grounds already have trees growing there. First, you've got to decide which, if any at all, should be removed. These would include, for example, small trees that interfere with the growth of larger ones, as well as dead trees. Then you've got to decide what kinds of trees should be added—if any. If you have no trees, then your job will be selecting the kinds you want (and are best suited to your property) and how many you want to plant.

In taking stock of your needs, you will want to make several important observations. Before drawing up your plan, this checklist will be of value:

- Locate water and sewer pipes, septic systems, and underground utility lines.

- Locate overhead utility wires and cables.

- Determine low spots where water normally collects and remains for lengthy periods during wet spells. Also, try to learn what the level of the water table is in your location.

- Determine which are the south, west, and north sides of the house.

- Decide what your present and future plans are for improvements—such as a patio, garden, swimming pool, or extension.

- If sidewalks and curbs are not in, try to determine where they will probably be placed.

- If your home hasn't been built yet, review the plans. Determine where it will be situated on the plot, and what its size and style will be.

- Determine whether construction equipment can get in and out of areas where you intend to have work done.

- Identify by name all existing trees.

- Try to learn where natural rock ledges, if any, are located beneath the surface.

- Ask yourself if any of the existing trees contribute to the interest of the grounds or form a frame for the house.

- Decide whether two or more of the existing trees appear to interfere with the growth of others.

ε❧ BLUEPRINTING YOUR TREE LANDSCAPE PLAN. Seldom are two properties alike, except, perhaps, in some developments. But in beautifying a plot, everyone has tastes of his own. We could not begin to explain to everyone who reads this book what trees are best to plant and where. First of all, this is a matter left to individual judgment and to private likes and dislikes. Second, not many types of trees can be grown easily anywhere in the country, since climate, weather, type of soil, and other factors vary. Therefore, we can only guide you with ideas: the actual decision-making is up to you.

In mapping out a plan, keep in mind that you want maximum results with minimum effort. So before you do any manual work or have it done, develop your plan carefully. Try to estimate what it will cost. Ask yourself if it will accomplish what you want, and be in the best interests of your property. Show your plan to the nurseryman from whom you intend to buy your trees, and get his opinions and advice. Some nurseries, incidentally, have landscape architects who can draw up plans for you if you buy from them. If your objectives include comfort, privacy, beauty, food, and value, it may be helpful to you—as a starter—to drive around your neighborhood and see what some of the local homeowners are doing with their trees. And while you're at it, take a pad and pencil along to jot some notes.

In blueprinting your plan on paper (see Figure 3), you will have to decide which trees you want to remove, what you want to add, and where you should place them.

8 WHICH TREES TO REMOVE. Unfortunately, live trees sometimes have to be removed—dead trees *always*. Some trees may be growing in places where you intend to build or develop; some may block the path necessary for use by construction equipment; and others might interfere with the growth of other trees or have roots that pose a threat to waterlines, pipes, septic systems, and even your house itself.

Before you conduct a wholesale removal of live trees, it is best to decide which you need out of the way *immediately*. There is good reason for letting the others grow for as long as possible; later you may get ideas that differ from today's. For example, you may decide that a spot under an old shade tree will serve as a fine picnic nook and that it actually appeals to you more than the patio you always tried to find time to build.

Sadly, the time may come when you must sacrifice some good trees now growing in good areas. You may, for example, find it necessary to open up a right-of-way for construction machines to do work on your grounds. But it may be best to leave such trees growing until the time actually comes. Plans do change.

To choose between two or more trees interfering with one another, you will probably want to retain the oldest and healthiest looking. But in doing so, be sure that the one you're saving is one not likely to contract a difficult-to-correct disease such as Dutch elm disease—which, by the way, has severely diminished the numbers and threatened the extinction of our beloved American elm. In choosing the favored tree, also consider characteristics such as the projected height at maturity, the rate of growth, and the color.

Judgment must be exercised. To illustrate, suppose two interfering trees are growing fairly close to your house. It would probably be best to remove the one nearest the foundation, since its roots and branches may pose problems as they grow toward the building.

Figure 3

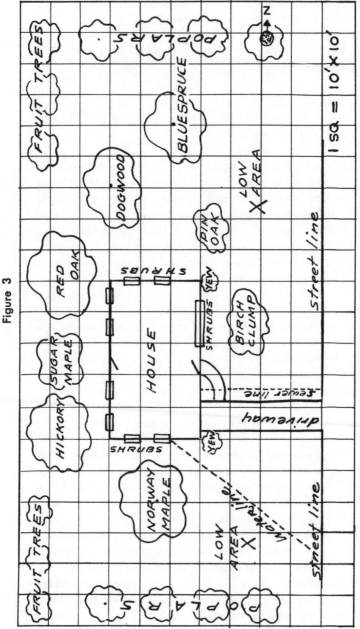

FRUIT TREES

POPLARS

N

BLUE SPRUCE

DOGWOOD

LOW X AREA

RED OAK

PIN OAK

SHRUBS

YEW

SUGAR MAPLE

HICKORY

HOUSE

BIRCH CLUMP

SHRUBS

Sewer line

driveway

SHRUBS

YEW

NORWAY MAPLE

LOW AREA X

Water line

Street line

FRUIT TREES

POPLARS

1 SQ = 10' X 10'

Street line

BLUEPRINTING THE PLAN

How graph paper may be used for planning your plot. Show proposed trees as well as existing trees; also indicate locations of water and sewer lines and other points where plantings should be avoided. Consider spread of foliage at maturity when positioning new trees.

Every effort should be made to avoid future problems, often costly ones. Trees growing too close to houses have cracked foundations, clogged water and sewer pipes, marred the sides and roofs of buildings, and threatened the safety of occupants during storms; tree roots have produced the cave-in of concrete-block septic tanks. You can see how important it is to determine which trees are likely to cause such problems!

When a tree seemingly has to give way to construction, don't forget, too, that one way to save it—and you should, unless it will pose an insuperable problem—is to make changes in your building plans. For instance, if the installation of a driveway or sewer line necessitates destroying a beautiful oak, perhaps the work can be done elsewhere on the grounds. In short, save what you can—both trees and money.

ε➠ WHERE TO PLANT NEW TREES. As we mentioned, trees around the home are most useful for comfort, privacy, food, and beauty (as well as value). Let us discuss these four benefits, one at a time.

The comfort of our home contributes much to our love for it. In the heat of the summer we want to be cool; in the coldness of win-' ter we want to be warm.

Shade trees serve best in the summer when they are placed on the south and west sides of the home, where sunlight is strongest. Even when the home is air-conditioned, shade trees help. The house will be cooler, and electric bills will be less. Shade trees also preserve game areas, and shade patios and picnic nooks.

Coniferous trees (that is, cone-bearing trees such as hemlocks and pines, which do not lose their foliage in the winter) are useful both in the winter and summer. When they are on the north side of the home, they serve as windbreaks, and help cut heat bills. But be cautious about their use on the south and west sides, especially when they cover windows. They'll give you shade during the hot months, but during the cold months they'll cost you money: sunlight can help your furnace in its job of warming the house.

Several years ago, a couple who had moved to their new home found that sunlight pouring into the living room during the summer afternoons usually caused the inside temperature to rise to around ninety degrees. So they planted a shade tree (Norway maple) twenty to twenty-five feet from the picture window. Today, the height and breadth of the tree is sufficient to provide shade, helping to keep the house cooler on hot days.

In planning for shade—deciding where to plant your trees—it is best to find out where the sun will be at the time of the day you actually require shade. But remember that the position of the sun varies from day to day at a given time. For example, the location of the sun at 2:00 P.M. on July 23rd will differ greatly from where it was on March 15th at the same hour.

Our comfort also depends on the peace and quiet around our homes. A screen of trees, strategically placed, can do much to deaden neighborhood noises, especially the drone of automobile traffic. Such a screen will also protect the house and its occupants against wind and dust.

Privacy, too, is greatly desired. Because we do not want anyone peering into our windows, we draw the blinds at night. Similarly, we look for some privacy for our backyard gatherings, which may be accomplished by appropriately planting a few trees to form a screen. As a view for your guests, such a screen might also be a great improvement over, for example, a busy street.

To obtain beauty, you should virtually aim to produce a picture —one that will stop passersby, and interest them. The design should reflect your feeling of what your grounds require. Begin by standing in front of your property as you would to paint a picture. Study your problem. Ask yourself where you would place both ornamental and shade trees to give your lot the right touch. Your objectives should include framing the house properly, planting a variety of trees reasonably spaced, providing for color adequately, and selecting trees that—at their matured height—will conform to the size of the house. The trees you are including in your plan for shade and screening should also be a part of your design.

Tall trees, or trees that someday will be tall, if planted behind the house will eventually help give your home a pleasant setting against a background of foliage. Trees placed at the sides will help to frame the dwelling.

As already indicated, trees at maturity vary in height and spread. (See Chart B.) If you have a house the size of a mansion, you will want trees that grow tall. If your home is of average size—a split-level, ranch, or Cape Cod house, for example—trees of medium height would be about right for you. For a small place, it is desirable to plant small, slow growers rather than those that are likely to get out of hand eventually.

There are hundreds of types of trees from which to select. Many should be adequate for your purposes and wants. If you are planning to use something from the evergreen family, be sure you can handle it easily; some spruce, pine, and fir trees, for example, may not be suitable for the average plot because they grow to such immense heights, ultimately posing a safety hazard. But they do form ideal backdrops or settings for a big home. Hemlocks, which also grow tall, are better because they can be pruned regularly to keep them from getting out of hand.

If you're thinking along the lines of fruit and nut trees, these are most appropriately placed in a sectioned-off area in a corner of your plot. The soil should be good, and full sunlight on every tree is required for the best fruit production when the time for bearing comes.

When making your plan, don't forget to allow for lawn space and shrubs on the grounds. They are also an important part of your complete landscape picture. If you overplant, such openness can be easily lost.

Other points worth considering when developing your plan are as follows:

- Trees are useful for hiding unattractive views, such as errors in construction, rain leaders, outside electric and water meters, and bottled-gas tanks.

- Trees are useful for accenting corners of buildings or yards.

- Trees are useful for softening blank walls.

- Trees can be used effectively to enclose a garden or lawn area, a patio, and a clothes-drying yard.

- Several evergreens in a row (as well as flowering shrubs) can be useful as a hedge.

- Trees of varied heights and types help avoid monotony, and add to interest and variety.

&ᴗ WHAT TREES TO ADD. When you choose a tree for your grounds, there are important considerations besides price:

- The purpose for which a tree is intended. Do you want trees for shade or beauty or both? Do you want them to serve as part of a screen?

- Stature. Is it straight and symmetrical in shape?

- Hardiness. Will it easily survive drought spells? Will it have trouble growing in poor soil? Will the bitter winter winds damage it or stunt its growth?

- Resistance to disease and insects. Will the tree be constantly threatened by garden pests? Will you spend countless sums to keep it well sprayed?

- Cleanliness. Will the tree cause your grounds to look messy with fruit, blossoms, twigs, cones, seed, and bark, as well as leaves?

- Root habits. Will the roots of the tree, like those of maples, compete with grass in the area?

- Branches. Are there at least several branches extending from a single central leader? Or does the tree have a double leader (Y-shaped) that may pose problems when the tree grows larger?

- Size at maturity. Will the tree eventually be too large for your property? Or too small for your purpose?

- Rate of growth. Are you looking for shade as fast as possible? Or do you prefer slow-growing ornamental trees?

- The colors it gives. Do you want bright colors in autumn? Or do you want colorful blossoms in spring? Both, perhaps?

- Fruit and nuts to eat. Are you the practical sort of person who likes to grow food and at the same time have trees?

- When its leaves bud. Not all trees leaf out at the same time in spring. For example, ash and hickory trees are slower than maples, willows, and other softwood trees.

Getting Started on the Work

Once you have your plan formulated, you are ready to get the job under way. The work usually involves four chores: cutting down trees, selecting tree stock, planting, and general care.

ᔔ 1. CUTTING DOWN TREES. You must determine if a tree is too large to cut down yourself. If it is, it may be wise to have a professional tree expert do the job, for he is trained to work safely. You can probably do the work yourself if the tree is small or even medium-sized, and if it is in an open area where there are no utility lines, structures, or other trees. But if you are not sure of what you're doing, *don't attempt it!*

However, if you insist on cutting down the tree yourself, the following information will be of some guidance. But please, exercise extreme caution!

Whether you use a combustion-powered chain saw, handsaw, or ax, you can usually make the tree fall in whatever direction you choose. At a point waist high on the side where you want the tree to fall, make a level cut (parallel to the ground) into the trunk. But don't cut deeper than one third the thickness of the tree trunk. Next, make a diagonal cut (on a 45-degree angle) above the parallel cut to remove a V-shaped chunk of wood. The next step is to fell the tree. To do so, on the opposite side of the trunk make a not-quite-so-level cut (cutting slightly downward toward the point of the V-cut). (See Figure 4.)

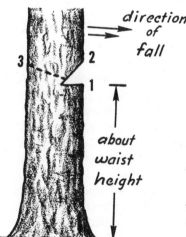

direction of fall

3 2 1

about waist height

Figure 4

The steps in felling a tree. Note that three cuts are made at waist height.

Before making any cuts, however, it may be wise if you use a long heavy rope tied at some point in the upper third of the tree to guide, from the ground, the falling of the tree.

Remaining tree stumps can be removed later in grading operations. You can saw them off below the grade level or dig them out entirely. Some chemicals, available on the market, are useful for simplifying the job of stump removal.

ॐ 2. SELECTING TREE STOCK. Two ideal sources for the trees you plan to grow on your plot are the woods and local nurseries.

Many different kinds of trees grow wild in wooded areas. Such trees can usually be transplanted to your property with success, but there are some problems in doing so. Most important, you will want to be sure that you have the permission of the landowner before you dig up any trees. The best time for transplanting is in the early spring, before the buds open.

To dig up a tree, first shovel a trench in a circle around the tree a little bit farther from the trunk than you estimate one half of the diameter of the rootball will be. (Refer to Chart A in estimating.) Then, with the back of your spade, cut away enough soil to form the ball as perfectly as possible. Sever all roots showing beneath or at the sides of the ball. Tip the tree to one side, and place the burlap beneath the ball; then tip the tree in the other direction, and place the burlap under that side. In doing so, use extreme caution to prevent the ball from falling apart. Finally, wrap burlap about the whole ball, and secure it tightly.

Actually, your best source of trees is a reliable nursery. When you buy trees, it may be to your advantage to know you are dealing with a reputable nurseryman, one on whom you can depend. In shopping for trees, don't be influenced by price alone. Consider quality, too. For example, a ten-foot maple tree costing more than another ten-foot maple could be a better buy, and often is. How can you tell? You should compare the characteristics of each—their symmetrical shapes, stature, branches, and the number of buds, for instance. You can also be guided by the standards of the American Association of Nurserymen. (See Chart A.)

Trees sold at nurseries come with their roots balled and burlapped or in cans. Some may be sold bare-rooted. Evergreens should never be moved bare-rooted; they should always be balled or in a container.

It might be useful to know what the policy of your nurseryman is (although this is not so important as the condition of the tree you're considering). For example, some nurseries deliver. Some will plant for you at additional cost. Some guarantee that the tree will "take" within a given period.

In dealing with a local nurseryman, you can also get some helpful advice. Ask questions before you make your selection. Learn what he carries and what he recommends on care after the tree is planted. The trees he sells, incidentally, will usually be the ones most suitable for your area, and they come in different sizes and shapes. Look them over well. When you select, it may be best to start out with a large tree if it's shade you're after. It will cost more; but, because trees do take time to grow, a larger one will give you benefits much sooner.

੨ 3. PLANTING. Tree planting is an art. If you do it yourself, you'll get a real workout. With small trees you may not mind the effort, but with large trees consider having it done for you or get some help. In any case, choose a bright cool day for the work if you can.

Essentially, tree planting involves eight steps (see Figure 5):

1. digging the hole
2. preparing the soil
3. setting the tree in the hole
4. watering
5. pruning back
6. filling the hole with soil—and allowing a basin
7. staking
8. guarding against sunscald and winter freeze

To describe the process in detail, you first have to dig a hole wide and deep enough to accommodate the rootball or bare roots of the tree.[1] Don't be stingy when doing this—roots need space to grow as well as good soil to feed on.

Allow for about 9 inches of clearance completely around the ball. For example, for a rootball 24 inches wide, make your hole 42 inches wide ($24'' + 9'' + 9'' = 42''$).

[1] In figuring the required size of the hole needed for a bare-rooted tree, try to estimate the size of the rootball such a tree would have if it were balled. (See Chart A.)

Figure 5

HOW TO PLANT A TREE

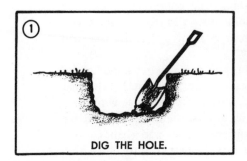

DIG THE HOLE.

PREPARE SOIL, POSITION TREE.

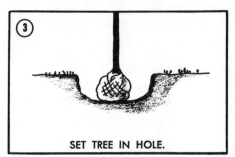

SET TREE IN HOLE.

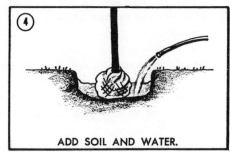

ADD SOIL AND WATER.

PRUNE BACK.

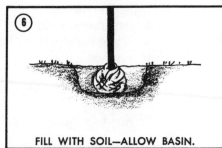

FILL WITH SOIL—ALLOW BASIN.

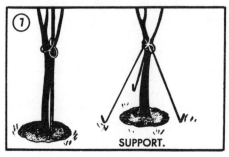

SUPPORT.

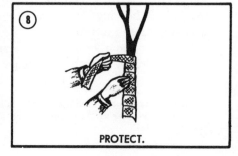

PROTECT.

The depth of the hole will depend on what the size of the ball and condition of the soil are. Sometimes the quality of the soil where a tree is to be planted may be poor. It may contain too much clay (which can mean inadequate drainage) or it may contain too much sand (which can result in an insufficient amount of food on which roots depend for nourishment). You may find, when digging, that the earth beneath you is full of rubble. In any case, it will be important to provide a "pocket" of good soil in which the tree's roots will have plenty of food and freedom to grow.[2] A good way to determine the depth of the hole is to make it one and one-half times the height of the rootball. For example, if the height of the rootball is 18 inches, the hole should be 27 inches deep ($18'' + 9'' = 27''$). This is 9 inches deeper than the rootball needs. The extra depth—9 inches —is filled first with 4½ inches of peat moss, then topped with 4½ inches of a mixture of rich topsoil and peat moss.

The next step is to set the burlapped rootball of the tree in the center of the hole. Keep in mind that the base of the tree trunk must be at the same ground surface level that it was before it was dug up. Open the burlap at the neck and pull back slightly. If the rootball has been wrapped in canvas, or anything besides burlap, remove it *entirely*.

If you are planting a bare-rooted tree, before setting the tree in the hole form a tepee-shaped mound of soil centered at the base of the hole. Rest the tree on the peak of the mound, permitting the roots to spread outward and downward in the hole. The size of the earth mound should be governed by the proper level the tree should be. Before the bare-rooted tree is finally set in the hole, it may be wise to examine the roots. Any broken roots should be pruned off with pruning shears at a point just above the break. Be careful not to injure the delicate root hairs, since these are important to the tree's nutrition and growth. The more tiny root hairs there are, the stronger the root system—and, consequently, the better the chances for that tree's "taking" during the first year.

Fill the rest of the hole (around the rootball or bare roots) with good soil. While doing so, soak the hole with water to assure firmness and to eliminate air pockets around the roots. Prune the top of the tree to compensate for the loss of any roots during the trans-

[2] Additional information about soil is covered in the next chapter.

planting process. Some nursery-grown trees will not require pruning back; your nurseryman can guide you on this matter if you'll
ask him at the time of purchase.

When pruning is needed, cut off those portions of branches that
interfere with or crowd out other branches or those branches that
keep the tree from having a perfect symmetrical shape. When snip-
ping off branches, use a pair of pruning shears. It is best to cut just
above the nearest bud (that is, the side of the bud *away* from the
trunk of the tree). How much of the tree to cut back will depend
on the amount of damage you believe the root system suffered when
it was dug up. It may be safe—rather than assuming wrongly—to
cut back the uppermost branches by about a third.

After the hole is filled to the top, scoop away sufficient dirt in a
wide circle above the root zone to form a saucer-shaped basin. This
will facilitate the collection of garden-hose and rainfall water, and
make future feeding easy. It will also simplify mowing the lawn
around the tree. Fill the saucer-shaped basin with peat moss.

All newly planted trees need to be given some support to prevent
damage by wind gusts. A straight wooden stake about a foot longer
than the height of the tree, and sharpened at one end, should provide adequate support for small trees. Place the stake as close as
possible to the tree and drive it into the ground. But in doing this,
be careful not to disturb the root system. Secure the tree to the
stake with wire, as illustrated in Figure 5, but use a small section of
rubber or plastic hose as a cushion between the wire and trunk at
the lower branches. For larger trees, three guy wires staked to the
ground and attached to the tree in similar fashion should give adequate support. After about a year, the roots will be able to take over
the supporting job, since they form a perfect natural anchor as they
grow outward.

The next step is to provide for some protection against the elements of weather.

Young trees—especially thin-barked trees such as dogwoods,
beeches, and maples—are susceptible to a drying out of the bark on
the side exposed to sunlight. This is called "sunscald." It happens
mainly because of sudden exposure to the sun and because the roots
have not had a chance to establish themselves in the new spot. Since
some trees with thicker barks are also subject to sunscald, it is necessary to keep the trunks of most newly planted young trees well protected—at least for two or three years.

To prevent sunscald, we suggest the following procedure: From the base of the tree trunk simply wrap burlap, cheesecloth, or thick crepelike tree paper spirally upward to a point just above the lowest branches. This wrapping should not be removed until protection against sunscald is no longer considered necessary, probably when there has been sufficient new bark growth to allow natural protection.

Some trees, usually of the shrub variety, are subject to freeze damage during the first few years of growth. Protection may be afforded by shielding the tree from wind gusts with a burlap screen. Special sprays are available, and may be needed repeatedly during the winter months.

ठ◆ 4. GENERAL CARE. Your final work will be the general care that should always continue as the tree grows. During its first year of growth observe your tree closely. Water the tree copiously whenever it doesn't rain for a week—except when the ground freezes. There is no need to fertilize at the time you plant your tree, but some *well-rotted* cow manure spread in the "saucer" just before the ground freezes in the late fall or early winter will be helpful in providing the food your tree needs. In addition, fall-planted trees should have a thick mulch placed in the "saucer" to protect the root system from sharp changes in temperature.

The specific chores so necessary for the proper care your trees will need in the future are explained in the chapters that follow.

DO's and DON'T's

When Blueprinting the Plan

Monotony in landscaping may be avoided by planting trees of various heights, variously spaced.

Avoid the tendency to overplant.

Do not locate your trees in low areas where water is likely to collect during wet spells. The soil should have good drainage.

Don't place trees too close to each other. Otherwise, they will eventually interfere with each other's growth. (Refer to Chart B for the estimated breadth at maturity.)

Don't locate trees such as maples and willows near sidewalks, the house foundation, or sewer and water pipes.

Keep shade trees as far from the house as possible to avoid damage by growing branches in later years.

Take note of the shade that the tree you plan will cast as it grows. Too much shade will pose lawn and garden problems.

When Planting and Transplanting

Early spring before the buds open is the best time for planting and transplanting trees. Transplanting can also be done in the late fall.

Moving a tree is expensive. Know its characteristics before transplanting.

Avoid injury to roots as much as possible.

If there are broken roots, snip off the hanging part at a point very close to and above the break. Use pruning shears.

Never allow the roots of any tree to dry up. Protect from the sun.

Never transplant an evergreen without first balling the roots, unless planting is a matter of moments away.

Before digging the hole, set the tree in place and decide the exact position it will be when planted.

Don't plant trees too deep or too shallow.

Be patient the first season with transplanted wild-growing trees. Normally, they don't adjust to a new environment as a nursery-grown tree does.

When the tree you're planting has a double leader (Y-shaped), cut one leader off to get it started right, or consider cabling (see Chapter 7).

Miscellaneous

Be cautious of competition that some trees give grass.

Cover your newly planted fruit trees when heavy frost is expected to avoid possible injury to buds or blossoms.

Avoid placing outdoor barbecue pits and fireplaces where smoke or heat will do harm to nearby trees.

When shopping for trees, a three-foot tree with good roots is far better than a six-foot tree with roots in mediocre or poor condition.

Avoid the use of salts (for melting snow and ice in the wintertime) near tree-root zones.

If you lose a tree, replace it at the earliest opportunity.

Safety Tips

Wear gloves and proper clothing to avoid hazards such as poison ivy, oak, and so on, insect and snake bites, and skin scrapes.

Learn what poison ivy looks like, and avoid it. Never burn it. (Poison-ivy leaves are green and glossy in summer, reddish in fall, and grow in clusters of three—sometimes up the trunks of trees.)

Be careful when you use an ax or other cutting tool.

Be sure children and others keep a safe distance when you're doing your work.

Get help in lifting heavy objects. If you must lift, use the leg muscles—not your back muscles.

Flag stakes and guy wires to warn passersby who cross your lawn. Ordinary white rags will do.

3 SOIL—THE PRIME SOURCE OF TREE NOURISHMENT

The Story Behind Soil

Some people think of soil as simply "dirt." But to the homeowner-gardener it is that part of the earth's crust in which, depending on its quality, vegetation grows. Understanding the important part soil plays in the growth of trees requires some basic knowledge of soil itself.

ও ITS ORIGIN. A long time ago—many millions of years ago—the natural ground on which we stand today looked much different from what it does today. Theories hold that as the crust of the earth cooled, it turned to solid rock. The action of water, winds, frost, heat, ice in the form of glaciers, and later even plants, all had a role in cracking and grinding up the rock into boulders, gravel, and sand. These smaller particles contributed increasingly to the abrasive power of the wind and water, resulting in even finer particles. Decayed organic matter in the form of plant and animal remains, when mixed with the loose, fine particles of rock, generally enabled the retention of moisture and warmth, and completed the chief ingredients of soil as we know it now.

Consequently, we can assume that the soil today is the result of a slow, natural process taking many thousands of years. It is evident, therefore, that the soil on your property is a valuable asset.

ও THERE ARE DIFFERENT KINDS OF SOILS. A visit to a virgin woodland will disclose beneath the trees a rich, dark-looking soil. Such soil, often used as topsoil, contains what we call "humus." Humus is made up of moisture and dead organic matter—the decayed remains of leaves, twigs, tree stumps, animals, and other formerly living things. Yet in beach areas, such as those on Long Island, we would find pure sand, that part of soil remaining after the continuous beating of the ocean has removed all other elements. The soil, of course, differs according to regional environment.

Let's examine the three common types of soil, one of which is likely to be what you have on your grounds. All may or may not contain some organic matter, the life-giving element.

Sandy Soil. This is composed of loose particles, and is porous to water and air. Since it will not hold water for long, it is subject to quick drying, especially in periods of drought.

Clayey Soil. This is a compact, hard soil through which water drains into the ground slowly, passage of air is restricted, and the normal penetration of roots is prevented. Sometimes referred to as "hardpan," this type of soil is usually found at depths of from fifteen to eighteen inches—sometimes as much as three feet.

Loamy Soil. This is an in-between type of soil, or a mixture of clay and sand. It gives adequate drainage and ventilation, and if it contains organic material it is ideally suited for growing trees.

In your ground, there are probably different layers of soil. The most common are topsoil (at the surface), subsoil (below the topsoil), and, finally, hardpan. The topsoil is most fertile because it contains bacteria—millions of microorganisms—that influence tree growth. Some degree of fertility in subsoil may be due to organic matter washed by rain from the topsoil downward.

Hardpan, which is hard in texture, not very rich organically, and impervious to water, is sometimes fatal to trees. (Hardpan is hard because it has been packed for hundreds of years.) When the roots of a tree grow deeper into the ground, they sometimes come into contact with hardpan. The lack of elements there could starve the roots, and the hardness could hamper their development; trapped water could drown them.

How to Tell the Quality of Your Soil

As we pointed out, soil is composed of minute particles of weathered rock and humus. A number of elements present are also vital to plant growth. Among the most important ones are *nitrogen*, necessary for growth of new tissue and of the healthy green found in leaves; *phosphorus*, for root growth; *potassium* or *potash*, for the manufacture of sugars which contribute to the tree's resistance to disease and cold weather; and *calcium*, for the development of bacteria in the soil as well as development of roots.

Other elements important to proper plant nutrition are carbon, hydrogen, oxygen, manganese, boron, sulfur, iron, copper, magnesium, zinc, and molybdenum. Most of these are usually found in a soil of good quality. The only exceptions are carbon, oxygen, and hydrogen, which originate with water or air in the growing process.

Lack of calcium causes the soil to turn sour, or *acid*, thus reducing the number of helpful bacteria. An abundance of calcium means that the soil is sweet, or *alkaline*. Soils are classified as either *acid*, *alkaline*, or *neutral*. The latter implies a "happy medium."

There is a system of measuring the amount of acidity or alkalinity present in soil. We talk of the temperature outdoors being so many degrees Fahrenheit. Similarly, we measure acidity and alkalinity in terms of the "pH factor." Fourteen major units compose the pH scale: pH_0 to pH_{14}. (See Figure 6.) Midway, or pH_7, is the neutral point. Pure water is said to be neutral, neither acid nor alkaline. From pH_0 to pH_7 indicates acidity. From pH_7 to pH_{14} indicates alkalinity. Most trees grow in soil neither too acid nor too alkaline, but trees do have preferences. (See Chart F.)

There are three ways of determining what the condition of your soil is: the hand test; do-it-yourself chemical analysis; and analyses by agricultural experts.

᠙᠊ 1. THE HAND TEST. A good, productive soil usually looks dark in color, and crumbles apart easily when dry. When wet, it can be molded into a neat mudpie, creamy and smooth in texture. A clay soil can also be formed into a mudpie, but it is not creamy in texture. When dry, it does not break apart easily. A sandy soil will not hold together to make a mudpie. Determining nutritional value of soil by this method of inspection is somewhat difficult, and a chemical analysis is suggested.

᠙᠊ 2. DO-IT-YOURSELF CHEMICAL ANALYSIS. There are three ways of testing for calcium content (acidity-alkalinity). First, you can buy an inexpensive soil test kit, which contains instructions for its use. Or, if you prefer, you can mix samples of soil with a litmus solution and allow it to stand. If the liquid turns bluish in color, the soil is alkaline. If it turns red, the soil is acid. Intermediate tones indicate a reaction closer to neutral. Finally, blue litmus paper can be

Figure 6

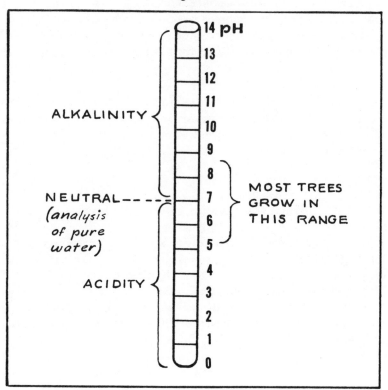

Acidity and alkalinity are measured in terms of "pH factor," as temperature is measured in terms of "degrees."

used in still another method of analyzing soil. When brought into contact with wet soil (mud) within twenty minutes it either changes in color or remains blue. A quick change to red suggests acidity and the lack of calcium.

ᘍᕀ 3. ANALYSES BY AGRICULTURAL EXPERTS. Chemists and field representatives of agricultural chemical companies can test your soil to determine its content. In addition, most counties have United States Government agricultural agents who will test the acidity or alkalinity of soil as a public service. Usually the cost is nominal, and you can find out what you need to do to improve the soil.

The agricultural agent may also be able to tell you whether a soil survey report has been published for your county and, if so, where you can find a copy.

&❧ How to Test for Other Chemical Elements. Soil test kits are available in many garden stores and nurseries for determining whether important elements are present in your soil, and in correct amounts. They are inexpensive and easy to use.

How You Can Improve Your Soil

Many of the minerals vital to soil are usually contained in the finely ground-up particles that were once rock. The carbon and oxygen are provided by the tree itself when the leaves "breathe." Hydrogen is provided by the water taken in at the roots. But sometimes it is necessary to help the soil along by providing it with its most important chemical elements: calcium, nitrogen, phosphorus, and potassium.

&❧ How to Increase the Alkalinity of Soil. Assuming that we've already tested our soil for its sweetness or sourness, let us assume that the soil is very sour, or acid. To sweeten it, simply add to it a sprinkling of lime (which is largely composed of calcium). Available by the bag in hardware and garden stores, lime neutralizes acid reaction, encourages earthworms to visit and aerate the soil, and speeds up the decomposition of organic matter. (When added to a sandy soil, it hastens the breakup of sand particles into smaller fragments.)

Be sure, however, not to overlime, as this tends to affect such minerals as iron, manganese, and magnesium, and makes them less available to the tree. Sometimes the overuse of lime will "lock up" the soil, preventing the release of nitrogen. The amount of lime to use depends on the type of tree you're planting; most trees like a slightly acid soil and some slightly alkaline.

Larger trees are generally able to control the acid-alkaline content of the soil they grow in because their leaves drop in the fall, and then decay and mulch into the ground containing the feeding root hairs. Oak trees, for example, like a sour soil; when oak leaves decay into the ground they cause the soil there to be sufficiently acid to make any oak tree growing there happy.

However, lime does not permanently correct soil acidity. Rainfall can cause lime to wash into the ground, and eventually acidity will reappear near the surface.

ॐ How to Increase the Acidity of Soil. This may be accomplished either by using a leafmold composed of decayed oak leaves or with a mixture of nitrate of soda. Work it thoroughly into the soil. Rainfall will help promote acidity; after the first rain, test the soil for proper acid content.

ॐ Providing for the Lack of Nitrogen, Phosphorus, and Potassium. Fertilizers—natural and commercial types—normally contain all three of these elements. Natural (organic) fertilizers may be in the form of an animal manure, compost (which is decayed vegetable and animal remains), or humus. Commercial (inorganic) fertilizers can be bought at hardware and garden supply stores as well as at nurseries.

ॐ Animal Manure. The most useful of all organic manures is animal manure. The composition and value of the manure depends on what animal was the source. Here is a typical analysis showing the differences:[1]

100 lbs. OF MANURE OF THE	WATER (lbs.)	CONTAINS DRY MATTER (lbs.)	NITROGEN (oz.)	PHOS-PHORUS (oz.)	POTAS-SIUM (oz.)
cow	84	15	7.68	2.4	7.6
pig	85	14	6.08	3.04	6.72
horse	74	25	10.72	4.32	9.12
sheep	66	33	23.36	6.88	12.16
chicken	55	44	20.8	12.8	14.4

Adding any such manures to your soil improves its physical structure and texture. Fresh, or green, manure should be left to decay

[1] Stanley B. Whitehead, *Gardener's Earth* (J. M. Dent & Sons, Ltd., London, 1945), p. 100.

before putting it to use, as its richness has a tendency to burn. The drier it is, the better. When in a state of decomposition, it adds to the microorganic population of the soil, resulting in multiplication and colonization of soil bacteria.

The value of using animal manure rather than commercial fertilizer has to do with its organic matter and water-holding capacity. In addition, it promotes bacteria and other organisms in the soil, and causes earlier warming of the soil in the springtime.[2]

To apply animal manure, break up and turn over the ground around your smaller trees, between a point just inside and a point just beyond where the tips of the outside branches extend and overhang. Set the manure on the surface in the fall, and allow it to weather during the winter. In the spring, work the manure into the ground with a spade. By then, melting snows and rainfall will have washed bacteria into the ground to the root system.

ೋ COMPOST. One way of quickly transforming organic materials into that which will promote the richness of soil is "compost-making." This will cost you practically nothing, and with a minimum of effort you can have a good organic fertilizer within a year. It will probably amaze you that much of the garbage you ordinarily dispose of—including leftover foods, weeds, and even vacuum-cleaner dust—can be used to manufacture your own fertilizer, or "compost." Here's how:

Select a spot on your property that has fairly good drainage, or at least where water will not collect. Determine how much ground you wish to use for this do-it-yourself project. The authors would recommend something like five by five feet as a starter.

Mark your area, using stakes or string, and dig a pit within this area to a depth of roughly a foot. Level the base of the excavation, and do *not* line it with stone, brick, or wood, since it is important that free access is allowed for worms and soil bacteria, which are helpful in compost making. The soil removed, if of good quality, should be set aside for later use.

To begin, place a twelve-inch layer of coarse material, such as foundation prunings and wilted flowers, inside your excavation. With your spade, chop up these materials as much as you can.

---

[2] Growth of most trees resumes when the temperature of the soil rises to above 40° F.

Figure 7

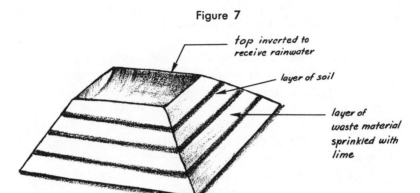

The completed compost heap: pyramid-shaped, covered with soil, the top is shaped to catch rainwater.

Sprinkle the layer with lime—just enough to make it look like a very light snowfall. Above this, place two to three inches of a good-quality soil, and soak with water. To this, add a layer of whatever else you can contribute to the heap.

The following lists suggest suitable additions to your compost pile:

From Your Grounds	From Inside the Home
plant remains	vegetable stalks
leaves	bread
grass clippings	vacuum-cleaner sweepings
foundation trimmings	leftover foods (cooked or
farm refuse	uncooked)
wilted flowers	pieces of wool
animal manures	peanut shells
pine needles	rinds
twigs	human or animal hair
weeds	wood ash
tree prunings	sawdust
straw	
hay	
clover	

Make this layer five to twelve inches in thickness, the precise amount depending on the condition of the material. For example, dry, coarse material should be twelve inches in thickness, and fine, moist material five inches.

Next, sprinkle very lightly with lime, add another two inches of a good soil, and soak with water. Above this, place another layer of material, sprinkle lightly with lime, add more soil, and so on.

Occasionally, mix some manure or peat moss, or both, in with a layer of soil, but when doing so omit the sprinkling of lime on the layer of material directly beneath it. The reason for this is that lime can be harmful to organic matter in manure.

Everything added to the heap should be moist, but not wet. Dried-out materials should be moistened before being placed on the heap.

The heap should be shaped somewhat like a pyramid as it is built. (See Figure 7.) The entire outside should be covered with soil. Always make the top slightly concave to catch rainwater. Never allow the heap to dry out; to keep it moist, sprinkle it with the garden hose in hot, dry weather. After about six or seven months, remake the entire heap, turning it over with a spade, and rebuilding it in the form of a pyramid. Do this once every two months after that.

In roughly a year the heap should be fully decomposed. To fertilize the soil above the root zone of your tree, spade the compost into the ground in the same manner as that described in the preceding section on animal manure.

ଽ HUMUS. This also can be purchased at stores selling garden supplies, or you can pick some up yourself in any wooded area. The decomposed leaves beneath the trees are called "leafmold." This is considered to be a very rich humus.

ଽ COMMERCIAL FERTILIZERS.[3] These are the fertilizers that have been chemically balanced to meet the needs of your trees. They contain nitrogen, phosphorus, and potassium (potash) in amounts to meet your specific needs. Manures are not balanced fertilizers. How

---

[3] Commercial fertilizer is more fully described in the next chapter, which treats the feeding of trees.

manure and commercial fertilizer differ in content is illustrated in
the following table: [4]

100 LBS. COW MANURE		100 LBS. COMMERCIAL FERTILIZER
7 oz.	nitrogen	9 lbs.*
7 oz.	potassium	9 lbs.*
2.5 oz.	phosphorus	3.2 lbs.*

* Mixtures of commercial fertilizers vary, and are labeled on packages ac-
cordingly.

ಶಿ IMPROVING AERATION AND DRAINAGE. The working in of organic
matter or peat moss will open up the close texture of soil to permit
aeration and drainage. This is covered in more detail in the next
chapter.

ಶಿ THE IDEAL SOIL FOR YOUR TREES. The best soil is one neither
too clayey nor too sandy. (See Chart E.) It should be a combination
of both to allow for good drainage and aeration; and, of course, it
should contain organic matter. This is usually soil that shows no
signs of puddling at the surface, and does not dry out too quickly
between rainy spells.[5] A soil that fits this description and is at least
fairly dark (not necessarily black) is probably good for growing
trees. Also of importance is the pH factor, described earlier.

A good soil also contains minerals, dissolved and undissolved;
decaying and decayed organic matter resulting from the presence of
plant and animal remains; and a population of living organisms, including fungi, bacteria, earthworms, and insects—all in constant
activity.

Study your soil periodically, and if you find it necessary to make
improvements, allow a full year for the purpose. A good way of
protecting your soil is by growing grass, plants, and other vegetation. This will prevent damage to the soil by the sun and by weather-
ing. If your soil contains the vital elements, and is getting whatever
attention it may need, your trees should have little or no trouble in
getting their proper nutrition.

[4] F. F. Rockwell, *10,000 Garden Questions* . . . (Doubleday & Co., Inc.,
Garden City, N.Y., 1944).
[5] To test your drainage, dig a hole two to three feet deep, and watch for
signs of puddling in the hole after a heavy rainfall. If water does not collect,
consider the drainage adequate.

Providing trees with the food they need is discussed at greater length in the next chapter.

DO's and DON'T's

Improving Soil Condition

Don't add lime to a newly manured soil; it is best to wait at least six weeks.

Mulches around the bases of trees help keep the soil uniformly moist, even during dry spells.

When using manures for fertilizing, be sure it is well rotted. Green or raw manure will burn roots if it is placed near them.

Don't allow your soil to become too sour. This will cause the useful bacteria to diminish.

Gypsum (calcium sulfate) sprinkled on a heavy-textured clay soil will help make it more crumbly. The best time to do so is just before the spring rains.

Never overlime.

Making a Compost Heap

If you are making a compost heap, allow for aeration at all times. Punching holes in different parts of the heap will allow air to penetrate freely.

When adding to the compost heap, if some materials are wet it might be helpful to include some peat moss.

Locate your compost heap in a remote spot on your property.

Miscellaneous

Taking a sample of soil for testing by your county agricultural agent must be done accurately. Check with him in advance to learn what the required procedure is; also, ask him for mailing containers if they are available.

Try to prevent excessive water from collecting in soil by providing satisfactory drainage. Most trees will not thrive in a saturated soil.

4 FEEDING YOUR TREES

The Four Essential Ingredients for Tree Growth and Health

Good soil, as discussed in Chapter 3, represents only a general idea of what a tree needs. More specifically, there are four basic elements on which a tree depends for life and health. Aside from proper climate, season, and care, if you were to consider a tree's important requirements in order to survive, you would probably list *food, water, air,* and *sunlight.* All are of equal value to a tree, and the omission of any one or more could spell death for the tree. The importance of these elements cannot be stressed enough. Supplying your trees with these elements could be the key to owning a healthy, flourishing tree.

In the forest, nature provides trees with all the nourishment required. This is made possible through the decay of fallen leaves, twigs, plants, and animals on the forest floor.

Trees on home properties do not have the same ideal conditions, however. Carefully manicured lawns contain no mulch or compost. The ground hardens as the result of pedestrian traffic; it also dries out quicker than a soil covered with humus and other decayed matter. Consequently, special care must be exercised by the home-owner.

All four elements, if present, work hand in hand to promote tree growth, to encourage improved bloom for the following year, to stimulate strength, and to give resistance to damage by insects and disease.

Perhaps the following experience will help to illustrate the importance of these elements:

One of the authors has a hickory tree in his yard that shows signs

47

of weakening every other year or so. He recalls one year in particular when no leaves or buds appeared on the tree until June. At first he paid little attention to this phenomenon because hickory trees are usually late in blooming. But when the neighboring trees—including two other hickory trees—were filled with leaves, he decided something was wrong.

He determined that the tree was still alive by scratching the bark and noting that it was green underneath. Further examination showed that the ground below the tree was hard and dry. (The soil in the area is generally clayey.) It was obvious that the soil around the tree's root system contained little in nutrition. The tree was badly in need of food, and in addition it was probably not receiving enough water and air.

The author referred to the four elements as a checklist: Is the tree hungry? Is it thirsty? Is it having trouble breathing? Is there adequate sunlight?

Let us discuss these four elements, one at a time, relating their importance to the affected tree.

&> Food. In the first and third chapters we learned that a tree feeds on the soil through its rootlets—the fine hairs extending from the root system below the surface of the ground. When a soil contains little or no bacteria and moisture, the tree growing in it will probably go hungry.

The author's objective with the hickory tree was to get food, in a constant supply and in the proper proportions, to the root system. He employed a method familiar to tree experts in feeding trees.

First, he used a crowbar to bore holes in the ground—eighteen inches apart—in a ring around the trunk at the extreme end of the longest limbs. (See Figure 8.)[1]

Next, he filled the holes two thirds full with commercial fertilizer. On top of this, dirt was added to fill up the holes. Basically, this constitutes the feeding process. It represents what generally is done to feed most any tree artificially.[2]

---

[1] When punching feeding holes in a good lawn, drive the crowbar into the ground diagonally to lift a small section of sod. Then drill straight downward. This permits the section of sod to be used for sealing up the hole without spoiling the appearance of the lawn.

[2] Some successfully use liquid fertilizer for foliage feeding.

Figure 8

To feed a large tree, punch holes 15" to 18" deep in a circle around the tree at the drip line, as illustrated. A crowbar (or heavy-duty electric drill with auger bit) is normally used. Holes should be spaced about 18" apart.

ৡৣ THE USE OF COMMERCIAL FERTILIZER IN FEEDING. Commercial fertilizer is a manufactured tree food containing chemical elements that are essential to satisfy a tree's great appetite. Commercial fertilizer may be purchased by the bag, in cans, or in bottles at almost any garden supply shop. It usually comes in powdered form, but may be bought in liquid form as well. Its purpose is to provide for the easy and inexpensive application of nutrition when natural food is not present.

Another advantage of commercial fertilizer concerns the three elements it contains—nitrogen, phosphorus, and potassium (potash). These elements are in balanced portions, to meet specific needs. For instance, since shade trees require mostly nitrogen for the development of foliage, a commercial fertilizer containing more nitrogen than phosphorus and potassium may be necessary.

⋙ THE ELEMENTS OF NITROGEN, PHOSPHORUS, AND POTASSIUM. Nitrogen is necessary for the growth of new tissue and of the healthy green found in leaves; phosphorus is essential for root growth; potassium is necessary in the manufacture of sugars that contribute to the tree's resistance to disease and to cold weather. All functions are, of course, important. But if one is of greater importance to a particular tree, you can purchase a fertilizer properly balanced to meet your requirements.

Every container of commercial fertilizer you buy has a set of three numbers that indicate in what proportions the nitrogen, phosphorus, and potassium are balanced. For example, suppose a bagful of fertilizer is labeled with the numbers "4-16-4." This means that:

> 4 percent of the fertilizer in the bag contains *nitrogen*
> 16 percent of the fertilizer in the bag contains *phosphorus*
> 4 percent of the fertilizer in the bag contains *potassium*
> ___
> 24 percent

From these figures we can tell that this mixture is high in phosphorus content, indicating that such a mixture would be particularly strong for root growth. The other 76 percent of the bag content, incidentally, is a carrying agent such as vermiculite—a mineral substance used to make a lightweight fertilizer.[3] When planting a tree, 5-10-5 is a good mixture to use—but *use it lightly if the tree is a small one* (that is, a tree that has a trunk less than two inches thick at a point one foot above ground level).

Of course, if you are feeding a tree, and no one function is more important than the others at the moment, then a mixture labeled "7-7-7" is good. This contains an equal amount of each of the three elements.

How much to feed depends on the size of the tree. The following table should be of some help:

[3] Formerly, sand was used as a carrying agent. It is still sometimes used.

How Much to Feed a Tree

TREE TRUNK (DBH) *	POUNDS OF COMMERCIAL FERTILIZER TO USE†
1"	1½
2"	3
3"	5
4"	6
5"	12
6"	18
8"	32
10"	40
12"	48

* Diameter, breast high.
† A simple means of weighing tree food is to determine how many pounds of fertilizer will be required for each hole. (Divide the number of holes you drill into the figure listed in the right-hand column above.) Use an empty coffee tin as a measuring-cup-type of container.

ও NATURAL FERTILIZERS. Natural fertilizers will do a good job of feeding your trees. In Chapter 3, we learned that natural fertilizers may be in the form of animal manure, compost made from decayed vegetable and animal remains, or humus. Natural fertilizers are usually obtainable from farms, but well-rotted cow manure can now be bought by the bagful in garden supply shops. There is also a liquid form of fertilizer, which is made from sheep manure mixed with bone meal and water; it is simply sprayed on the ground around shallow-rooted trees (such as maples, beeches, and dogwoods). Liquid fertilizer may also be injected into the earth in the parts of the ground where the outer root tips are located.

We know of two disadvantages of using natural fertilizer instead of commercial fertilizer. First, it has a tendency to burn the roots unless it is well decayed beforehand; in addition, you have no way of determining the balance of nitrogen, phosphorus, and potassium contained.

ও THE FEEDING SCHEDULE. The best times to feed trees are in late fall or in March. The job should be done at least once a year. Fruit and flowering trees could use one additional feeding just after the blossoms or fruit appear. Fertilizer will always be most effective when the ground is damp and the food is best able to work its way to the thousands of hungry little rootlets down below. The results of your efforts will be noticed in the spring when the buds begin blooming.

If you have many trees—particularly large ones—and you want to do the feeding work yourself to save money, you had better plan on an ambitious schedule. You'll need the better part of an afternoon to feed just one large tree. You may, therefore, wish to concentrate on the smaller trees yourself, and leave the big ones to a tree expert.

An ambitious schedule is of special importance when the soil conditions around your property are poor, such as when the ground contains a lot of clay.

Figure 9   FEEDING TIPS

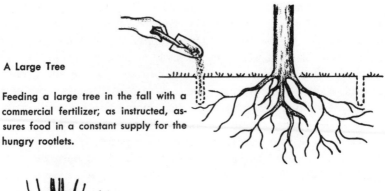

A Large Tree

Feeding a large tree in the fall with a commercial fertilizer; as instructed, assures food in a constant supply for the hungry rootlets.

A Small Tree

Manure mulch worked into the ground over the root zone of a small tree in the fall builds up the soil during the winter months. *Be sure the manure is well rotted* to avoid burning the root system.

ᖘ WATER. The author's hickory tree was also thirsty. After the food was poured into the holes and covered up, he turned on the lawn sprinkler to saturate the ground containing the root system. Once dampened, the food in the holes was activated. The actual feeding process had begun. Natural rainfall took over to keep the ground moist.

How much you have to water your trees between rainfalls depends on the circumstances that prevail. If you have a soil that holds moisture for long periods, natural rainfall alone can be relied on; you will be spared the trouble of watering. Sometimes mulch worked into your topsoil helps to keep the sun from drying out the dirt. A quick thundershower or a few moments of watering with your garden hose will never provide an adequate drink for your trees. In periods of drought, you may want to do what the author did with his lawn sprinkler.[4]

Young trees will probably need watering more often—a good soaking about the root system at least once a week. Very small trees may be able to get by with a couple of pailfuls of water each week.

THE CULTIVATED CIRCLE FOR SMALL TREES

To facilitate feeding and watering small trees, a cultivated circle (saucer-shaped) should be provided above the root zone. This guide may be helpful in determining what size it should be.

TRUNK THICKNESS*	RECOMMENDED CIRCLE DIAMETER
up to 1″	1½ feet
1½″	1½ feet
2″	2 feet
2½″ or more	2½ feet

* 12″ aboveground.

ᖘ HOW NECESSARY IS WATERING A TREE IN THE WINTER? Many trees—particularly evergreens and other shrubs—will be in serious danger and may possibly die because they do not get enough water during the cold winter months. Quite often, tree owners will blame the frozen weather for their losses. They may not realize that the loss, or near-loss, is due to the lack of water. Actually, the cold

---

4 Some people have successfully used hydrospears, which can be bought at most garden supply shops. They are inserted deep into the soil for quick watering where needed in the root zone.

winds during the winter months cause the evaporation of the water content of branches, leaves, and needles. Trouble results when the roots cannot find sufficient water to replace that which is lost. This is what causes the browning, dying foliage that you have probably noticed in the spring.[5] Thus the importance of watering, even in the winter. However, when the ground is frozen and the outside tap is turned off, watering is impracticable. Therefore, certain measures will have to be taken to protect your trees before the freezing weather sets in.

ૐ PROTECTING YOUR TREES IN THE WINTER MONTHS. It may be best to feed all trees in the late fall, since the potassium helps provide the tree with resistance to cold weather. Small trees and shrubs, in particular, should be protected against the icy blasts of wintry winds.

For many years property owners have draped burlap or plastic sheets on the side of specimens where the winter winds are liable to come from. This has proved to be effective as a means of keeping the winds from blowing directly on the plantings. Protection against the blasts of icy winds ensures against fast evaporation of the water contained in branches, leaves, and needles. Such protective measures have saved many trees and shrubs from loss.

In recent years, a special spray—obtainable at garden supply shops —has given the same protection as burlap and plastic. A hardened film coating on the branches and needles serves as an invisible wind-breaker, and seals in moisture. The coating melts and evaporates when warm weather arrives.

Another measure that the homeowner may want to consider involves placing a well-rotted animal manure above the entire root zone of small trees, shrubs, and shallow-rooted trees. Doing this in the late fall will help keep the ground moist and warmer than usual during the winter, in addition to providing nutrition.

ૐ AIR. In punching feeding holes around his hickory tree, the author opened "pathways" for air to flow freely in the root zone. The holes also made it easier for water to penetrate downward. (The clay in the soil contributes to its hardness.)

Trees must have air to breathe, not only aboveground but below as well. A root system that does not receive a constant supply of

[5] The loss of newly transplanted stock in the winter may be due to the inability of the damaged roots to replace the evaporated water as fast as it is lost.

air cannot function properly. There must be a free circulation of air, and this is made possible only by a porous soil. For this reason trees will not survive when they live in a waterlogged soil.

By the same token, where new houses are being constructed heavy equipment is likely to tamp down the soil around trees, cutting off the air supply the roots need; in addition, a hard-packed soil makes it difficult for rainwater to penetrate the ground.

When soil is of poor quality, as it was around the author's hickory tree, it may be wise for the tree gardener to plug up the feeding holes with peat moss, sand, or charcoal instead of a clayey dirt. This should permit continued aeration.

It is also suggested that when planting a tree, allow for adequate drainage and a good porous soil about the root system. (See Figure 5.) Take into consideration the conditions that would exist in all seasons. For example, determine if water will collect at a low spot and remain for long periods during the rainy season. More than one tree has been lost by overlooking this fact.

ﾇ❧ SUNLIGHT. Sunlight is also important in the feeding process. The food elements absorbed from the soil by the roots are converted into nutrition in the leaves on contact with CO_2 and sunlight. Trees can manage nicely with a bit of sunlight during the day, but they should really have as much as possible. The value of sunlight is evidenced by the longer branches that sometimes appear on one side of a tree—the sunnier side. In the forest, many trees are extremely tall, with branches and foliage only at the very top where the sunlight is. If they sprout branches partway up, it will be due to rays of sunshine that regularly find their way through the thick overhead umbrella of leaves.

When you plant your trees, consider the sunlight your tree will get as it grows. Keep it apart from nearby trees, since eventually they could block the sunlight. Shadiness can hamper the growth of a tree, so never overlook the value of sunlight.

How to Tell When Your Tree Needs a Feeding

Trees sometimes show symptoms of malnutrition. When they do, these should be taken as signs that food, water, air, sunlight, or combinations of these, are desperately needed. The following checklist will be useful to you; it illustrates what to look for if your trees are trying to tell you a meal is overdue. Your tree needs your immediate attention:

when it appears to be dying back (loss of leaves at very top)
when the foliage on its crown is thinner than usual
when its leaves are prematurely off-color
when dead limbs are readily noticed, possibly abundant
when its leaves are smaller than usual
when twigs grow shorter than usual
when it is damaged during house construction
when insects are invading
when disease has struck

DO's and DON'T's

At Feeding Time

Don't overfeed. An overdose of tree food could burn the roots, resulting in possible loss of the tree.

Before punching feeding holes, soak the area under the tree a day or two ahead with water from the lawn sprinkler. This will make the job of boring much easier.

Roots restricted by driveways, walls, and buildings may need to be fed more often. Caution may have to be exercised, however, to avoid burning the roots.

Avoid fertilizers heavy on nitrogen for feeding newly planted trees during their first six months. A *light feeding* of a commercial organic fertilizer is adequate at the time of planting.

Don't overfill feeding holes with fertilizer. Grass will grow taller and faster in those spots if you do—and may eventually die.

Avoid spillage of fertilizer on the lawn. It will cause burning of the grass where spilled.

In the Summer Months

A mulch of straw, peat moss, sawdust, or wood chips placed around the base of your tree above the root zone will help to hold moisture in the soil.

Water generously in hot weather—but not on the foliage.

Five Ways to Feed a Tree

1. Punching holes in the root zone with a crowbar.

2. Broadcasting dry food on the surface of the ground below a tree prior to rainfall.

3. Injecting liquid food into the root zone.

4. Liquid foliage spraying.

5. Trunk injection, entailing the drilling of holes into the sapwood and inserting tubes and pressurized capsules of fertilizer. (This can be done only by a certified tree expert.)

Safety Tips

Be kind to your hands! Use gloves when you are drilling holes with a crowbar.

When you are punching feeding holes, spread your feet to avoid injury.

Get help in lifting heavy bags of tree food.

If you must lift, do not use your back muscles. Use your leg muscles; bend your legs, not your back.

Be on the lookout for poison ivy—and avoid touching it.

When you are not working, put your tools in their proper places to prevent accidental stumbles and possible injuries.

5 PRUNING—THE KEY TO TREE HEALTH, VIGOR, AND BEAUTY

Why Prune?

ξ❧ WHAT IS PRUNING? For the same reason most men visit a barbershop periodically, trees also have to be clipped and trimmed: for the sake of appearance. But more important, the pruning of trees also includes the removal or cutting away of dead, diseased, rubbing, and interfering branches. Careful attention to this need plays a key role in the future health and growth of trees. Both health and growth are important to the beauty and value of your home and grounds.

ξ❧ THE NEED FOR PRUNING. Though a young tree may require some initial care to make it look attractive and symmetrical in form, it will probably need very little pruning at such an early time. But as it gets older, changing conditions may affect the tree, putting it in need of thoughtful trimming. Branches die because of lack of food and water, sunscald (caused by repeated destruction of foliage by insects and fungi), the work of borers, or disease. Then, too, windstorms, ice storms, and other acts of nature sometimes leave in their wake torn, hanging branches of all sizes. In time, deadwood rots, and rotting usually spreads to other parts of the tree. In addition, trees suffer bark injuries caused by animals, construction equipment, and insects.

All these factors point to one very important thing: decay or rot must be prevented. This is done by removal of deadwood. Branches, for example, should be cut off when they die or are damaged; and special care must be given at the point where the branch was removed.

Pruning is done for a number of reasons:

- Cleaning up. Dead and decayed wood are breeding places for insects and disease.

- Appearance. A beautiful tree is one with a well-balanced shape.

- Proper growth. Branches that interfere with other branches and block proper amounts of light and air may have to be eliminated.

- Safety. Broken and dead branches are a hazard to person and property.

- Transplanting. In moving a tree from one place to another, the crown of the tree is pruned to offset the loss of tiny root hairs, and broken roots are cut back to healthy wood.

- Opening vistas. A view may be obtained without entirely sacrificing a tree that obstructs the view.

- Line clearance. Some branches may eventually become a menace to telephone and electric wires. (Have this pruning done before the utility *must* do it—for they may "scalp" your tree.)

- Correcting storm damage. Reshaping of what's left of a tree damaged by a storm may be necessary.

- Improved fruit production. Your fruit trees can give more and better-quality fruit through pruning.

Doing the Work

𝒞❧ MATERIALS YOU NEED FOR PRUNING. For best results in doing your own tree-surgery work, you may want to equip yourself with a few tools and supplies. Taking safety into consideration, here are our general suggestions if you have both large and small trees:

Hand pruning shears—suitable for clipping small trees and evergreens.

Pruning saw. This has a curved blade, and is used where larger limbs and twigs are generally too thick for hand pruning shears.

Pole-type pruning saw—for the hard-to-reach limbs when you're in the tree or on the ground. This really is nothing more than a saw, similar to the above, attached to a long pole.

Figure 10 TOOLS NEEDED FOR PRUNING

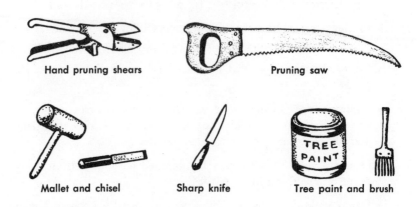

Hand pruning shears   Pruning saw

Mallet and chisel   Sharp knife   Tree paint and brush

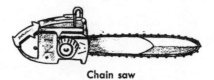

Pole-type pruning saw

Chain saw

Portable chain saw—for heavier-than-normal work such as cutting off large limbs and taking down large trees.

Chisel and mallet—for tracing (trimming) bark wounds or digging out cavities on the tree trunk. The size of the wound should determine the size of the chisel used.

Sharp knife—for finishing the tracing work on bark wounds of certain types of trees.

Tree paint—if you wish to dress bark wounds and limb cuts for the sake of appearance.

It is important to remember to keep all cutting tools sharp. Doing this will assure clean, neat cuts. This is of real importance to the speedy healing of tree wounds.

It is also necessary to sterilize your tools after working on an infected tree, such as one with Dutch elm disease. This should help prevent the spread of disease to other trees. Sterilization can be accomplished simply by using any cleaning fluid, such as alcohol, to wash the tools.

In selecting a tree paint, there are several different brands available. They are usually labeled "tree wound dressing" or "tree paint." Hardware and garden stores, as well as nurseries, ordinarily carry such paint.

If you should decide to paint for the sake of appearance, the paint you use should never be of the kind used, for instance, to paint a house. Tree paint should not crack when dried. It must not contain too much creosote, which is dangerous to the cambium, but it should permit the gradual escape of gases and moisture from inside the tree.

ৡ১ How to Prune. Before you actually begin to perform your first tree operation, there are a few principles you ought to know.

For cutting and trimming off limbs, there are three types of cuts: the jump cut, the flush cut, and the slanting topcut. There is a reason for using every one of these cuts in your pruning operations, particularly in big trees. (See Figure 11.)

ৡ১ Jump Cut. The jump cut is the combination of two other cuts known as an undercut and a topcut. Its primary purpose is to permit the pruning of a very heavy limb without disastrous results. Examining the illustration, you can readily see what would happen if you began pruning a heavy limb by first cutting through the top. Partway through, the weight of the limb would cause it to drop, taking healthy bark with it, and endangering other parts of the tree—and even your own safety.

By making a proper jump cut (first the undercut, *then* the topcut), you are able to guide, or at least plan, where your limb will drop.

ৡ১ Flush Cut. When the limb is removed, a stub will remain. This should be eliminated with a flush cut, and the reason is simple: When the wood of a stub dies, it begins to decay. Decay spreads, and can eat its way into the heart of the tree. Once that happens, you've got real problems, and may even lose the tree.

A flush cut, therefore, is nothing more than removing a limb at the point where it meets the trunk or, perhaps, a larger limb.

ॐ SLANTING TOPCUT. The only other type of cut you may be concerned with is the slanting topcut. In pruning, particularly with fruit trees, this cut is used primarily to restrict abnormal sucker growth.[1] This cut is actually made diagonally so that no flat surfaces remain. A slanting surface where the cut is made will permit quick drainage, or runoff, of rainwater. Leaving no place for water to collect is one way of preventing decay.

Figure 11 THE THREE PROPER PRUNING CUTS

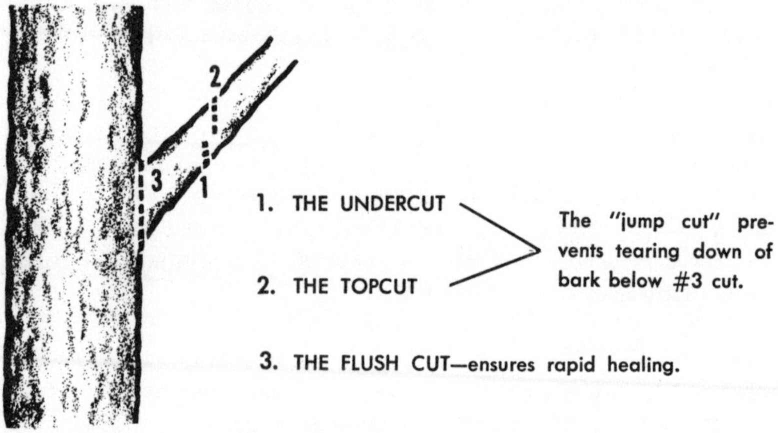

1. THE UNDERCUT

2. THE TOPCUT

The "jump cut" prevents tearing down of bark below #3 cut.

3. THE FLUSH CUT—ensures rapid healing.

These are the basic rules for cutting and trimming limbs and twigs. They are basically what professional tree men use, and the reasons for their importance to tree care should be apparent. The principles for pruning are simple, and if you, as the homeowner, bear them in mind, the rest is a matter of judgment and taste.

But when should you prune? How can you tell when your trees need pruning? All reasons for pruning come under one or the other of two classifications: *to correct* or *to beautify*.

ॐ WOUNDS TO TREE BARK. The trees on one of the authors' prop-

[1] Suckers are useless branches that very seldom produce fruit.

erty suffered much damage at the time his home was under construction. Large scrapes on the trunks of the trees—some injuries measuring as much as one by three feet—were evidence of the damage. Had treatment of these wounds been delayed, decay most certainly would have set in in time. But taking care of this condition promptly placed the trees on the road to recovery.

To treat a bark wound, use your mallet and chisel. Cut away the affected area, chiseling out a vertical, elliptically shaped piece of bark (like an egg standing on end), and bring the ends to sharp points. Be sure to trim away all loose bark. Make cuts neat and clean.[2] If possible, try to avoid cutting into the cambium. The shape of the elliptical cut makes it easier for water to run out. It also enables speedier healing of the wound. (See Figure 12.)

Polyethylene may be useful in preventing moisture at the exposed area, and encouraging rapid healing. If this is preferred, first trim the edges of the bark wound as described above. Then moisten the entire wound and cover with two layers of polyethylene. Secure the polyethylene padding with string or tape tied completely around the tree trunk. Polyethylene is obtainable in many hardware stores.

> PAINTING OF CUTS AND WOUNDS. In recent years, the long-used process of painting cuts and wounds has been discontinued by professional tree experts. Research has shown that painting affords no benefit to trees other than aesthetic value.

When one of your trees requires extensive pruning, you may find yourself removing hundreds of twigs and limbs. If you had to paint every cut, you would have quite a chore. You may, however, decide to paint several of the larger cuts to eliminate the "shiners," or exposed white wood. Actually, through nature's own healing powers, a cut or wound will darken by itself and blend in with the color of the trunk.

If a professional tree expert is doing the work for you, he will probably charge you more (for time and materials) if you insist on the painting of the cuts and wounds.

> USE YOUR OWN JUDGMENT WITHIN REASON. As a general rule, a good pruning job depends on the judgment of the individual do-

---

[2] On thin-barked trees, trim with a sharp knife. The use of a mallet and chisel on such trees sometimes loosens the inner bark from the tree, making a space into which insects and water may later find their way.

Figure 12

HOW TO TRACE AND TREAT A BARK WOUND

1. With chisel and mallet, trace out an elliptically shaped cut. On thin-barked trees, use a sharp knife. Cut only through the bark.

2. Bring top and bottom to points to allow for speedier healing, and provide for water drainage. Make cuts clean and neat.

3. If you wish, coat entire wound with tree paint. *(Never use a paint not intended for use as a tree paint!)*

4. Coating with tree paint will enhance the appearance. In time, as the tree grows, the wound should close up and disappear.

ing the work. After all dead and interfering branches are removed, you may decide, for example, to cut off additional branches for purposes of "thinning out" or shaping the tree. This may possibly include the cutting off of portions of branches that have a tendency to become too heavy. However, there are two things you will want to avoid when you prune:

1. Don't remove a live branch or foliage if it will expose part of the tree to sunscald.[3] Try putting the tree in your position; if you have a tender skin, a full day in the sun during the hot summer months—let us say, at the beach—will inevitably cause you to burn and later to peel. Similarly, this can happen to a tree—particularly tender-barked trees such as birches, dogwoods, fruit trees, maples, and lindens.

The healing powers of a tree are considerably slower than those of a human being. Decay could set in before the bark has had an opportunity to heal. One of the functions of tree foliage in the summertime is to protect the tree against sunscald.

2. Don't remove a live branch if it will cause disfigurement to the tree. Use your "good eye" when pruning. Stand away from your job now and then, and inspect your progress. Your object should be what you set out to do—such as giving your tree a symmetrical look.

Now that you know pruning is left to your judgment, don't get "butcher happy." In other words, don't remove too much foliage.

Another hazard in pruning too heavily is the subsequent growth of suckers (tiny twigs) that draw on food and energy vital to the rest of the tree. Fruit trees, in particular, suffer when this happens, and fruit production the following year could be seriously affected.

Other Pruning Chores

ঙ৯ REMOVING BORERS THAT DIG INTO THE BARK. Borers are wormy insects that eat their way into the bark of the tree, causing sufficient damage to kill the tree. Though they vary in size and appearance, they are seldom larger than a half to three fourths of an inch in length.

To detect whether such borers are in your trees, look for small

---

[3] Willow trees can be cut drastically to reduce their top-heaviness, and they will grow back very rapidly.

Figure 13

PROPER AND IMPROPER TWIG PRUNING

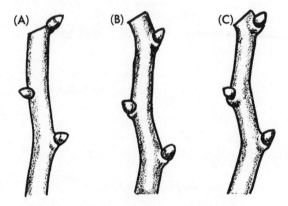

(A)　　　(B)　　　(C)

A and B illustrate improper twig pruning. In A, pruning was too close to the bud. This will cause the twig or branch to "die back" to the next bud. In B, too much of a stub was left above the bud. C shows a proper twig cut. No unsightly stub is left. Note that the cut is on an angle, to allow water and moisture to drain off.

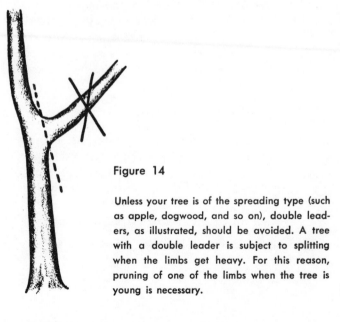

Figure 14

Unless your tree is of the spreading type (such as apple, dogwood, and so on), double leaders, as illustrated, should be avoided. A tree with a double leader is subject to splitting when the limbs get heavy. For this reason, pruning of one of the limbs when the tree is young is necessary.

holes in the bark. The best time for such an inspection is between late spring and early summer.

After hibernating in the soil during the winter months, these borers begin their disastrous work on trees in the spring.

REMEDY: (1) With a mallet and chisel (for large wounds) or a pen knife (for small wounds), trace out a vertical, elliptically shaped cut (following the instructions given earlier) in the general area of the trunk where borer holes are detected. Insert a flexible wire through each of the holes, and probe to kill the borer. (2) Inject borer paste (available at garden supply shops) in the burrows to asphyxiate the insect.

PREVENTION: Spray around the lower part of the trunk at the "flare" with diazinone in nearly spring and in the late fall before the ground freezes.

ੴ REMOVING GIRDLING ROOTS. You can almost always detect roots that cross over other roots and are exposed on the surface at the base of the tree; these are "girdling roots." Another indication of this problem occurs when the trunk grows straight down into the earth instead of flaring off as a trunk base naturally does. (See Figure 15.) Girdling roots are dangerous because in time they may choke off a tree, causing it to die.

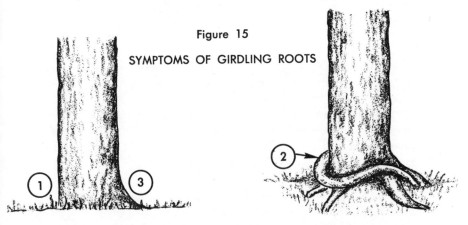

Figure 15

SYMPTOMS OF GIRDLING ROOTS

1. When the base of a trunk shows no indication of a natural "flare," such as #3, there may be a girdling root choking other roots underground.

2. When a root curls around the trunk, as shown, it may be choking or about to choke other roots above the ground level.

REMEDY: Simply cut through the root at any point as close as possible to where it connects with the trunk of the tree. (Use caution so as not to disturb living tissue on the trunk or on other roots.) This will free the trunk and other roots from being bound too tightly. If several girdling roots are apparent, remove only one or two the first year, the balance two years later.

PREVENTION: Guide young trees by checking periodically to be sure roots are not beginning to take on a "girdling" appearance.

ॐ REMOVING EMBEDDED OBJECTS. There are many stories about finding objects buried deep inside large trees. Such things as barbed wire, horseshoes, and even baby carriage wheels have been discovered after the trees containing them were cut down.

Gnarled sections of a trunk may indicate where the cambium of the tree has wrapped itself around such objects.

Embedded objects are most harmful to the tree when they are partially exposed on the surface of the trunk. Not only do they threaten their immediate area of the trunk with decay; they also hamper normal growth of the cambium. If undetected, they can also ruin the chain of a power saw when the tree finally has to be cut down.

REMEDY: Remove wire or object carefully, so as not to rupture the bark any more than is necessary. Treat the tree as you would for a bark wound, chiseling to shape, and painting to prevent decay.

ॐ RELIEVING WATER PRESSURE IN THE HEARTWOOD OF THE TREE. Sometimes a slimy, stagnant water will ooze through the bark or from a crotch. This may mean that excess moisture has built up in the form of pressure in the center, or heartwood, of the tree faster than the tree could expel it in normal processes.

REMEDY: At an upward angle, drill two or three holes at different points of the tree trunk in the vicinity of such oozing. In each of the holes, insert a pipe the diameter of the hole to enable proper drainage and to prevent oozing and discoloration on the trunk.

ॐ PRUNING IN CASES OF RESTRICTED ROOT DEVELOPMENT. The roots of some trees may have a limited area of soil in which to grow. This may be the result of the construction of a street, a wall, a sidewalk, or a building. Consequently, the tree could lose its leaves prematurely in the fall or there could be an overall weakening of the tree. (A tree with limited root area is the same as a house plant that becomes "pot-bound.")

REMEDY: To maintain a balance of growth in a tree with restricted roots, trim off parts of the uppermost branches (at the top and sides) of the tree. After pruning the branches, dig around the tree (no closer than where the new feeding line would be). In so doing, prune all exposed roots in order to "thin" excess wood in the root system. Return dirt to the trench after root pruning.

ɞ REMOVING "BLEEDING CANKERS." The sign that your tree is suffering from a so-called "bleeding canker" (it usually affects maples and oaks) is indicated by an oozing sap accompanied by reddish-brown discolorations in the cambium or inner bark. This infection can cause your tree serious internal trouble if it is not checked immediately. Although there is no definite control for this disease—at least not today—pruning may be the best method.

REMEDY: Cut away the infected area, preferably in freezing weather to control the flow of sap. Then trim and treat it as you would a bark wound.

ɞ REMOVING CHOKING VINES. Though some vines hanging from trees may appear picturesque, this could be at the expense of the tree. When vines grow to monstrous proportions, they can choke the life from a tree. Typical of this is bittersweet.

Poison ivy also grows this way, and makes the job of removal somewhat of a problem. If you discover, perhaps on first moving to a new home, that practically every tree is draped with poison ivy vines—some as thick as two inches—you should follow this plan. First, put on a pair of old gloves for protection; then sever (with a saw) each vine at its base close to the ground. Now disinfect the saw upon completion of the work to prevent the possibility of contracting poison ivy when you next use the saw. A year later, the dead, brittle vines may be easily removed.

ɞ VISTA WORK. Sometimes trees may obscure a pleasant view—perhaps a waterfall, a lake, the spires of a church, or a far-off mountain. The job of retrieving a view is one of judgment, and must be done to satisfy your own tastes and needs. But remember the principles of pruning, making sure that you don't remove a branch that will permit sunlight to focus strongly on the bark or cause disfigurement to the tree. Sometimes it may be necessary to remove entire trees, especially in a wooded area, but try to save them if possible. Cutting off lower branches or trimming the tops of trees is usually sufficient for a view, and you can still enjoy your trees.

Your Pruning Timetable Is Important

For most trees the recommended time for pruning is in the spring, just before the leaves begin to bud. However, any time during the dormancy of the tree (when there are no leaves) is almost as good.

For a number of reasons, it may seem simpler to prune in the summertime because then it's easier to tell which branches are dead and which ones are alive. Or perhaps your vacation comes only in the summer, and this is the only time you can spare for pruning. By all means, go ahead and prune away. But in the summer months you run the risk of insects and disease—which are inactive in the winter and early spring—hampering your work. See Chart G for a seasonal guide for pruning.

On the other hand, top-heavy trees and branches should be pruned in the summer so you can determine where to make your cut and still leave sufficient foliage to form the crown of the tree.

Now you may ask: How can I tell, in winter, which branches are alive and which ones are dead? Live branches always have buds. Dead limbs are usually a different color tone than the live, budded ones.

ֱ♥ DOGWOODS AND OTHER FLOWERING TREES. Dogwoods and other flowering trees should be pruned just after they blossom. Earlier pruning could delay budding of flowers as long as a year or more.

ֱ♥ MAPLES. All maples should be pruned during freezing, not thawing, periods of the winter because root pressure causes the various species of the maple family to "bleed" sap when a cut is made in its bark. Freezing temperatures, therefore, would permit making necessary repairs to the tree without loss of sap.[4]

ֱ♥ EVERGREENS. The recommended time for pruning evergreens is

[4] In the spring, these trees may show some unsightly bleeding, but it is very seldom that this means the tree has been permanently injured. Certain trees other than maples are also subject to bleeding.

July. If necessary, evergreens can be pruned in the early spring, before new growth appears, to correct winter damage.

Of course, in emergency situations pruning should be done immediately, regardless of season. Also, it is just as important to remove debris hanging from the tree immediately, thereby eliminating breeding places for insects and disease.

Good timing, as well as good judgment, is necessary for success in pruning. The earlier you begin, the better off you'll be in getting the results you want. Chart G should prove helpful to you in planning your pruning schedule.

DO's and DON'T's

Before Pruning

First, determine your pruning objectives. Then stand back and decide how you will do the job.

If you think the pruning job will be a major undertaking, consider calling in a tree expert.

Before undertaking a major task of pruning, it may be best to feed the tree the year before to bolster its health.

Pruning—General

Always begin a pruning job by eliminating deadwood and broken branches. Then prune tiny twigs growing at the base of the trunk, branches that rub one another, and branches that interfere with utility lines.

Remove broken limbs. Prune away stubs.

Avoid heavy pruning, particularly in fruit trees.

If the tree is on your lawn, remove some lower limbs, if necessary, to allow more light to reach the grass area and to make your mowing chores easier.

Use sharp tools, and avoid leaving rough edges when pruning.

Don't use ordinary paint or tar on your tree. Tree paint, or "tree wound dressing," is sold at many garden supply shops.

Palm Trees

To improve the appearance of palm trees, cut out oldest stems periodically. Prune as close to the ground as possible. Remove all seriously diseased leaves. When removing palm leaves, cut them from the underside to avoid tearing the fibers of the trunk of the tree. Never prune the terminal bud.

Other

Disinfect all tools after using them on diseased trees.

Never use climbing spikes to climb a tree that you're trying to save.

Safety Tips

Beware of poison ivy.

Be sure the ladder you use is not broken, and is secure before you climb it.

Never leave tools in a tree.

Keep children and others away from your work area until the job is done.

Avoid working near charged wires.

Be extremely careful in lifting, dropping, or lowering heavy branches.

Wear gloves, a long-sleeve shirt, and full-length trousers when working in a tree.

Exercise caution when you work with power tools.

Be careful in handling and using sharp tools.

Use a safety belt when working in a tree.

6 THE WAR AGAINST ENEMIES OF TREES

A Tree's Fight for Life

One of the authors noticed that a newly planted pin oak of his was not responding in the spring. All other trees in the neighborhood were filled with leaves for weeks, yet the pin oak was bare. It had had sufficient water. The soil used around its root system was of a good grade. The tree had been fed. The tree was a good specimen purchased from a reputable nursery.

From all indications, the trouble had to rest with an insect or disease of some kind. After a close examination, the author discovered what appeared to be tiny worms—gypsy moth caterpillars—hundreds on every branch. They were nibbling at the buds faster than the leaves could blossom. The tree was sprayed; the worms died; and shortly afterward the tree sprouted its leaves and blended in with the rest of the landscape.

This is typical of the kind of problem that trees face in their fight for life. Had the pin oak not been sprayed in time, it would have lost its power to produce leaves. Without leaves it would not be able to feed properly, because leaves are important to the breathing and food manufacturing processes during the growing season. The hot summer sun would have finished off the job, for without a protective umbrella of leaves the pin oak would inevitably suffer sunscald, and could die.

Trees ordinarily are susceptible to damage by insects and disease. It's best that the beginning gardener know what to expect, and be prepared to carry on whatever warfare is necessary when the time comes.

The Tree's Problems Explained

Usually insects attack in large numbers. Sometimes the damage to any one tree can be great. Sometimes it is slight. Often the damage goes undetected until it is too late to do anything about it. There are numerous kinds of insects and diseases in the United States that endanger trees. An attempt to list all of them would be confusing, but a brief discussion of pests in general will help the average person to understand what a tree has to contend with. Chart I will be of value to those who want to diagnose and correct their own insect and disease problems.

The tree's enemies may be placed in three categories: *insects, fungi,* and *scales.*

&ᐬ INSECTS. Not all insects are harmful to trees. As strange as it may sound, many are helpful. We shall discuss these friendly insects later in this chapter. See Chart H, "Who's Who Among the Bugs."

Harmful insects come in an assortment of sizes and shapes. The tiniest are microscopic in size. When insects are not visible to the naked eye, they are not usually identifiable by the layman. Even the experienced professional sometimes has trouble in this respect.

Some insects look like worms or caterpillars; others, like moths, beetles, grasshoppers, spiders, and ordinary bugs. Some are termites, which, as everyone knows, pose a threat to nearby homes. Many insects are airborne. Others crawl out of the ground and climb the trunks of trees. Certain insects favor specific types of trees, and rarely attack others. But nearly all trees are on the menus of one species or another.

Figure 16

A maple leaf torn to ribbons by insects

Figure 17

A maple leaf with symp-
toms of tar spot, a fun-
gus disease

Insects deform leaves, prevent buds from opening, and strip the branches of their foliage. Some insects (borers) tunnel into a tree trunk and eventually block the tree's lifeline that carries food up and down between roots and leaves. Some suck the vital juices from trees, and even live on the roots below the surface of the ground. Some cause unsightly galls, or growths, on leaves of deciduous and conifer trees. They turn the needles of evergreens brown. They ruin the edible fruits of fruit trees.

A menacing insect in recent years has been the gypsy moth cater-pillar (not to be confused with the tent caterpillar, notorious for its white tentlike webs in fruit trees). Devastating literally millions of acres of many kinds of trees in the northeastern United States, it is expected to be a perennial pest.

The gypsy moth caterpillar hatches in late April or early May from egg masses deposited the previous summer in shady, protected places such as the undersides of branches, beneath loose bark, in firewood, etc. Soon after hatching, these insects begin climbing to the tops of trees in response to light. They begin to feed by chewing small pinholes in leaves, and as they increase in size so do their appetites for the foliage.[1]

Every time an insect attacks, it contributes to the weakening of the tree, thereby making the victim tree more vulnerable to other pests that might finally kill it.

ॐ FUNGI. A tree is also subject to fungus diseases of many kinds. Sometimes a fungus is caused by insects and sometimes by excessive

[1] If a tree of yours is defoliated by this pest, chances are good that it will refoliate the same summer, especially if it's a healthy, hardwood tree. A com-plete defoliation will normally not kill a deciduous tree, but could be fatal to a conifer.

moisture, particularly in wet, rainy seasons. A fungus is an abnormal growth anywhere on the tree's bark, branches, or leaves. It is composed of microscopically small organisms. It may have the appearance of black scales or it may look like a moldy substance. In any event, fungus will cause fruit to blacken, and will defoliate shade trees, sometimes killing them.

A common fungus in the United States has been the Dutch elm disease. It has been traced to the elm bark beetle, which carries spores of the fungus from nearby infected trees and piles of wood to unaffected elm trees, on which they feed. In recent years, the American elm has experienced a discouraging record of loss because of this disease.

Fungi, which often results from deadwood or untreated trunk cavities, may also intensify problems. Consequences may be in the form of cankers—diseased and decayed areas of the trunk or branches that weaken a tree and make it liable to wind breakage.

The first symptoms of fungus diseases of the tree often appear on the leaves as tiny spots; in time, these enlarge. Eventually, the leaves may become disfigured, and drop prematurely.

ॐ SCALES. Another menace to trees is "scale." Scale is an insect that infects the trunk, branches, and twigs of trees. There are different kinds of scales, all of which obtain their food by sucking the juices out of the tree. The result is often a weakened tree that is, of

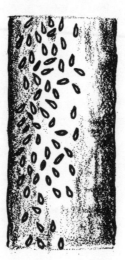

Figure 18

A tree trunk infested with oyster-shell scales

course, subjected to increased attacks by insects of all types.[2]

One kind of scale insect, for example, is the oyster-shell scale, which is from one eighth to one sixteenth of an inch in length, shaped somewhat like an oyster, and is dark slate gray in color. Another is the scurfy scale, which is round or slightly irregular in shape, about one twenty-fourth of an inch in diameter, and dirty white in color.

The cottony maple-leaf scale that normally infests only soft and sugar maples may be found on leaves as well as on twigs and branches. It has the appearance of a white, cottonlike wax coating.

What Can Be Done About Insects and Disease

Research over the years has uncovered a multitude of ways to control insects and disease. The most effective means has been through the use of chemicals, which are sprayed on or applied in other ways. But through natural means nature has already provided for the control of insects and disease—a field in which man is becoming more and more knowledgeable.

ຊ໐ THE USE OF CHEMICALS. On the market—more appropriately in nurseries, garden shops, and hardware stores—is a variety of liquids, powders, and other materials that can be used effectively to control many of the insects and diseases that endanger trees. Such chemicals fall into three classifications: *stomach poisons, contact poisons,* and *fumigants.*

ຊ໐ STOMACH POISONS. The most common stomach poison used by tree experts is Sevin. It is mixed with soap to ensure its sticking to leaves for long periods. The primary purpose for using Sevin is to poison the stomachs of insects that nibble at the coated leaves. The experts also use contact poisons in their spray programs.

Another type of stomach poison (not a chemical) is available to homeowners under the classification of biological controls. The most popular is *Bacillus thuringiensis,* commonly known as "Bt."

[2] Scale insects live off live (or green) wood.

&❧ CONTACT POISONS. Contact poisons, as implied, kill insects "on contact." They are generally safe for human beings on contact if the dosage is not excessive. Among the contact poisons sold are Sevin, malathion, methoxychlor, and miticides. Some of these chemicals are the ingredients of a commonly used liquid chemical marketed as "Isotox." Fungicides, obtainable in a wettable powder form, are another kind of contact poison, and are used to treat fungi. A fungicide is applied as a liquid spray or as a dust.

&❧ FUMIGANTS. A fumigant is essentially a wettable powder or liquid that gives off gas. One of the advantages of using a fumigant is that it will penetrate cracks, crevices, and hidden places that a liquid spray is not apt to reach. Among the fumigants available is Sevin.

&❧ VARIETY OF CHEMICALS AND EQUIPMENT AT YOUR DISPOSAL. Sprays are available in powdered form, and are dusted right onto the tree. Insecticides and fumigants sometimes are sold in combined form—thus providing a stomach poison for chewing insects, a contact poison for sucking insects, and a fungicide for various diseases.

Which chemical to use depends on the nature of the problem. Chart I, "Diagnosis and Prevention of Common Tree Insect-Disease

Figure 19

COMMON TYPES OF ECONOMICAL SPRAYING EQUIPMENT

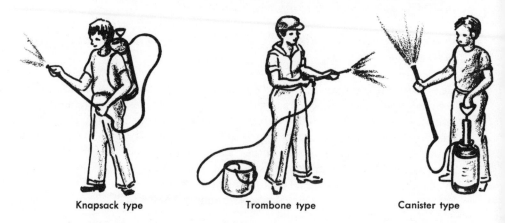

Knapsack type   Trombone type   Canister type

Sprayers can usually be rented if you don't wish to buy one. For heavy-duty work, a gasoline-engine-powered sprayer is available from farm supply dealers.

Problems," should be of substantial help. Your local dealer in pesticides can also advise you on what will be most useful to you. If the problem is an unusual one, your county agricultural agent may be of assistance. In any event, call on someone who is an *expert*, not a neighbor who may be just guessing at the remedy. Read your local newspapers and magazines, too, for information published on insects and diseases causing damage to trees in your area.

Chemicals are applied with special equipment that can be purchased or rented locally. For the average homeowner, any of various sprayers can be obtained economically, and can be used to spray small- and medium-sized trees. (It may be best to leave the larger trees to the professional tree experts, who are better equipped and experienced to meet large-scale problems.)

Applied sprays should be in the form of a fog or mist that drifts into the tree foliage and deposits a residue of moisture on the leaves. It may be best, first, to spray in an upward, diagonal direction from beneath the tree. Then encircle the tree from the outside to spray

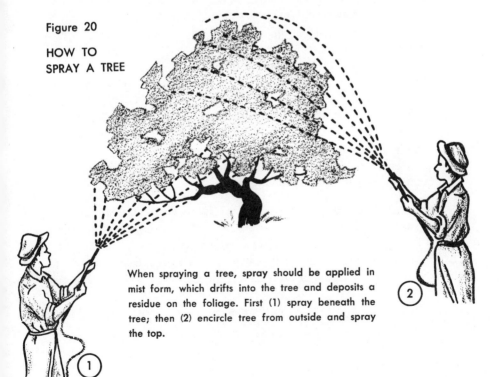

Figure 20

HOW TO
SPRAY A TREE

When spraying a tree, spray should be applied in mist form, which drifts into the tree and deposits a residue on the foliage. First (1) spray beneath the tree; then (2) encircle tree from outside and spray the top.

the top of the foliage. Be careful not to get chemicals in your eyes, nose, or mouth, and never spray against the wind.

Knowing the best time to spray will be of advantage to the beginning gardener. There are three occasions: (1) when you want to prevent trouble before it starts; (2) when an attack is imminent; (3) when insects are attacking.

When the insects are attacking, of course, damage may already have been inflicted. The result: leaves with a lacy appearance or branches stripped bare. This could—and often does—kill branches and twigs, making pruning a requirement, since deadwood attracts other harmful insects. But it is never too late to spray. The use of a contact spray can kill the culprits immediately, and thus prevent further damage.

It is often good to spray when an attack is imminent. This is usually when the caterpillar tents begin to appear in the crotches of nearby trees in the early spring or when the Dutch elm beetle is invading a neighborhood. But the surefire way to prevent real trouble is to plan a spray program before the problem has a chance to develop. Early spring is the best time.

First, before the buds open, a so-called "dormant spray" applied to the trees will control scale.[3] Dormant sprays are usually followed up with an "early foliage spray," applied after the buds have opened and when maple, oak, elm, and most shade tree leaves are the size of a twenty-five-cent piece. The early foliage spray—the most important spray of the year—should contain whatever chemical is recommended for your particular locality. Still another measure to take in the early spring is spreading a recommended chemical on your lawn to control grubs. This will help hold down the Japanese beetle menace during the summer.

ॐ PESTICIDE USE—A CONTROVERSIAL ISSUE. Pesticides, we have indicated, are the most effective means available in warring against the insects and the diseases that endanger our trees.

However, much discussion has taken place in recent years about the wisdom of spraying with chemicals. Certainly their use has met

[3] The dormant spray, containing a miscible oil, also penetrates the eggs of some overwintering insects, and searches out immature forms of other pests wedged in bark crevices or at the base of needles of conifer trees.

the objectives—namely, to rid trees and forest lands of insect pests. But, according to evidence in recent years, there may have been damaging side effects.

By her best-selling book, *Silent Spring*, the late Rachel Carson focused national attention upon this issue.[4] She contended that poisonous chemicals have been placed indiscriminately in the hands of spray-happy individuals who are unaware of the harm they cause. She explained in detail the poisonous properties of insecticides, and gave numerous examples of their effects on the health of man, birds, fish, and food supplies.

The evidence began piling up following years of spraying, especially with DDT and arsenate of lead. This is why these chemicals are no longer available for insect control purposes.

In one case, five years of intensive DDT spraying for control of elm bark beetles and mosquitoes virtually eliminated robins at Michigan State University, according to *Audubon* magazine.[5]

In Clear Lake, California, one thousand breeding pairs of a fish-eating bird, known as the western grebe, were drastically reduced in numbers, and for periods of years there was no reproduction activity whatsoever because of the use of pesticides, Robert L. Rudd, a University of California zoologist, said in his book *Pesticides and the Living Landscape*.

With the wide concern pesticides are causing today, it is conceivable that some chemicals will no doubt give way to other means of control. This leads us to the employment of other methods to control pests.

Already in use are organic substances—available in granular or liquid form—which can be sprinkled on the ground above a tree's roots, injected directly to the root zone, or sprayed onto its foliage. Although it's more expensive than the use of chemicals, this type of control is definitely less harmful to the environment.

Certainly we must agree that present chemical methods should not be permitted to continue if they are harmful. Our feathered and other animal friends should not be made to suffer. But we must also remember that neither should our good friends the trees.

[4] Rachel Carson, *Silent Spring* (Houghton Mifflin Co., Boston, 1962).
[5] Report by Dr. George J. Wallace appeared in *Audubon*, January–February, 1959. Copyright National Audubon Society.

ဗ‍ NATURE'S ROLE IN CONTROLLING PESTS. What nature provides for us is usually taken for granted. Not until the real facts are examined can we really appreciate all that has been placed on this earth to benefit and help us. Now we may be waking up. See Chart H, "Who's Who Among the Bugs."

The fact is that right under our noses, but without our knowledge, are biological and natural conditions at work trying to accomplish the same thing that we're trying to do with chemicals.

Everyone knows the role birds play. Since they gorge themselves on insects, they can be counted upon to do a share of the controlling job.

However, not all insects are pests. Nature maintains a good balance, and provides bugs to kill other bugs. In fact, the harmful insect's worst enemies are often its own cousins. From egg to death, most insects are surrounded by other insects that are trying to eat them or capture them to become food for their own developing brood. Among those insects helpful to man is the ladybug, recognizable by its hard orange turtlelike shell with black dots.

Another useful insect is the praying mantis, which looks something like an oversized cockroach. Under natural conditions, mantids —as they are called—feed almost entirely on insects that they capture alive. Most of their prey consists of insects injurious to vegetation. Unfortunately, there are also some useful insects on their menu, and, of course, they cannot be directed to a specific pest. But the good they do more than offsets the harm.

Research in the area of bug control by bugs continues. The federal government and some state governments have been spending large sums of money to come up with more effective ways of meeting the problem. The Entomology Research Division of the Agricultural Research Service, for example, even maintains laboratories in foreign countries to search for beneficial insects. When successful, using insects as a control is very economical and effective. For some types of insect pests, it may eventually replace chemical measures.

Disease also will curb the spread of insects. A bacterial disease known as "wilt" has destroyed gypsy moth caterpillars in large numbers; milky spore has affected the Japanese beetle by killing beetle grubs.

Climate, weather, and temperature also will control insects and disease. Wet spells in early spring have stimulated molds that have held down the population of destructive beetles. Late spring frosts have killed many larvae, and extremely dry summer weather has destroyed many insect eggs and killed newly hatched grubs. Soil type and the topography of land also tend to influence insect control through the limitation of vegetation on which the insects would normally feed.

Some trees have been noted as remarkably resistant to insects and disease. In Kitchener, Canada, for example, there is an apple tree that requires no spraying, since insects are not attracted to it. Even among the American elms, there have been trees that have successfully defended themselves against the deadly Dutch elm disease of recent years. But always remember this: *Regular and liberal feeding, pruning of deadwood, and favorable weather conditions can do much to keep a tree healthy and resistant to insect and disease damage.*

ॐ OTHER METHODS OF CONTROLLING PESTS. Aside from biological and natural means of control, experiments have been conducted in other ways. These have involved primarily the trapping of insects.

Some insects—such as Japanese beetles—are large enough to be handpicked from smaller trees. If you're not brave enough to touch them with your bare hand, try using a small stick to shove them into a can containing a half inch of kerosene.

In New York State, 13,000 traps—each consisting of a tin can, painted olive drab, containing sticky paper properly scented—were hung from the limbs of trees over a wide area; the principle was similar to that of flypaper. The purpose was to attract male gypsy moths in order to determine the location of insect pest infestation.

A more revolutionary means of trapping insects is through the use of a so-called "black," or ultraviolet, light. In North Carolina, experiments were conducted with such a light, and the result was a 58 percent reduction in eggs and larvae found on tobacco in one area.[6]

Food that gives off an odor attractive to insects has been used to lure pests into traps. Ordinary white lights have been employed for

---

[6] Now on the market is a variety of devices, such as traps and electronic "zappers," that capture or destroy insect pests.

years as a means of attracting insects to electrical wiring that then electrocutes them.

Banding the tree trunk with one of a variety of materials (such as a vegetable waxlike substance, special burlap, and polished tape) is an inexpensive control measure. A few years ago, one of the authors noticed caterpillars streaming out of a nearby tree containing the familiar caterpillar tents. A few of the creatures had managed to make their way to his trees for the express purpose of dining on the foliage. A band of waxlike substance placed around the trunks of the trees (about waist height) checked their advance.

Banding a tree with this sticky substance will prevent all kinds of crawling insects from invading. However, spreading it directly on the bark may have a few disadvantages: (1) it will leave an unsightly streak on the tree that could last for years, and (2) it could cause rot if left on the trunk for an indefinite period. For these reasons, it may be best to apply a band of cotton first, pressing it firmly to fill in all the crevices. Over this, smear the sticky material. (See Figure 21.)

Figure 21

A vegetable waxlike substance (one brand, for instance, is "Tanglefoot") is applied to a band of cotton placed around the tree to check the advance of crawling insects. The substance may be applied directly to the bark, but if left indefinitely it will cause rot on thin-barked trees. Otherwise, the dark-streaked band that remains may be objectionable in appearance.

The Spray Problem

If what's said in articles and private conversation about spraying worries you, perhaps listening to an unbiased opinion can ease your mind. You might try asking somebody who is neither in the business of spraying for profit nor fanatically against any chemical controls— someone at an experimental research center or local government extension service, for instance. In general, the chemicals available to the homeowner on the open market are considered to be safe when used as prescribed, although some persons with allergies could be subject to discomfort when making skin contact with or inhaling a direct spray. In any event, weigh the advantages of having a tree professional do your spraying for you.

Health Insurance for Your Trees

Here is a helpful ten-point health-insurance program for your trees. The "premium," in relation to the yield, is minimal:

1. Check for and eliminate dead trees, dead limbs, and piles of wood that may harbor termites and other harmful insects.

2. Are birds attracted to your property? They should be.

3. Check for limbs that are losing foliage, and dying. If there are any, trouble is brewing.

4. Do your neighbors spray when you do?

5. Keep your trees in a healthy, vigorous condition. This will ward off the effects of many insects and diseases. Feed them well.

6. Keep your trees watered during dry spells. Always keep newly planted trees well watered.

7. Look for cracks in the trunk bark caused by frost.

8. Look for tiny holes in the trunk that might reveal the presence of borers.

9. Look for spots or holes on leaves.

10. An early spraying of the foliage helps. A second spraying during the summer ensures.

DO's and DON'T's

General Spraying

Spray only when the outdoor temperature is in the 40°–79° range and when it is not expected to go higher or lower within the next twenty-four hours.

Don't spray indiscriminately. Read the instructions or get expert advice beforehand.

Don't drench trees when spraying. A fine mist is adequate.

Since the use of certain chemicals is forbidden in some locations, be sure to check your local laws before spraying.

Oil Sprays

Don't repeat a dormant oil spray during the same season.

Avoid using oil sprays during the summer months because they can cause "leaf burn" and change the flavor of fruits. The best time to use such a spray is in early spring, before budding.

Don't use a dormant oil spray on blue spruces and firs. Also, avoid oil sprays on thin-barked deciduous trees such as sugar and Japanese maples, beeches, butternuts, and walnuts. (However, a dormant oil spray may be used for such thin-barked trees if the oil is well diluted with water—1 pint of oil to 6 gallons of water, for example.)

Miscellaneous

Never use spray equipment that has been used to apply weed killer.

Don't allow "fly-by-night" tree sprayers to spray your trees. Use someone reputable if you cannot do the job yourself.

Don't leave the band of sticky substance used to trap insects on the bark of the trunk of the tree indefinitely; it can cause rot.

Never burn caterpillar tents in a tree.

Cut down dead trees to avoid attracting unwanted insect pests.

Prevent the spread of disease by sterilizing all pruning tools. (A wood or denatured alcohol is satisfactory.)

Safety Tips

Always read and follow directions on the labels of the chemicals you use.

Prepare your chemicals outdoors—never indoors.

Exercise caution in handling flammable chemicals.

Because of the possible danger of chemicals to the skin, wear a hat, gloves, long-sleeved shirt, and full-length trousers when spraying.

Never spray against the wind. Avoid getting chemicals in your eyes, nose, mouth, and open flesh wounds. It's suggested that you use a respirator.

Keep children, pets, and acquaintances away from where you are spraying until the job is done and until the spray has had a chance to dry. Persons with special allergies should plan to be away or remain indoors when spraying is done.

Avoid spillage of chemicals in pools of water where pets, birds, and other wildlife are apt to drink.

When storing chemicals, keep them out of the reach of children.

Label all chemicals properly to avoid confusion when you have to use them again.

If you must do any lifting, never use your back muscles; use your leg muscles. It's always better to get help than to take any chances.

7 SOME PRECAUTIONS FOR THE SAFETY OF YOUR TREES

Special efforts are sometimes necessary to safeguard your trees against certain natural and man-caused conditions posing a threat. These involve taking such precautionary measures as the following:

- protecting trees during periods of construction

- building a "well" when regrading is a necessity (to permit your tree to breathe properly)

- providing artificial support for trees weakened by various natural conditions

- installing protection against lightning

Be Cautious During Construction Operations!

The use of machines, such as bulldozers, on your property can unintentionally play more havoc with your trees than you think. To maneuver heavy-duty equipment about the average-sized plot requires elbow room. One slip can mean a sizable gash in the trunk of a tree. One forgetful moment can result in the weight of a giant machine packing down the soil over a tree's root system, cutting off its air supply, and making it difficult for water to penetrate. One faulty engine with dripping oil or gasoline also poses a serious threat to the condition of the soil.

There is the danger, too, of workmen unwittingly burning or piling refuse under a tree, nailing objects to the trunk, tearing off unwanted limbs, and damaging roots when digging. All these can mean serious consequences.

When planning any kind of construction in the vicinity of valuable trees, special care must be exercised in order to save them.

The first step, of course, is to determine which trees you want to save; Chapter 2 may be of some value here. In so doing, you will be making it easier for the workmen to determine the elbow room they need.

Next, build a fence around each of the trees you're saving. This can be makeshift and crudely fashioned; scrap materials will do very well. Your aim should be to block off an area of ground under the tree within the branch drip line. Whether this is accomplished with stakes driven into the ground or pieces of lumber nailed together to form a four- or six-sided wall, make your fence as sturdy as possible. (See Figure 22.)

"Well" Your Trees When Regrading Is Necessary

Sometimes construction work will require regrading to raise or lower the level of the ground. But disturbing the soil above the root

Figure 22

A crudely fashioned fence will protect both the ground above the root zone and the tree itself during construction operations on your grounds.

zone of a tree can have serious consequences: it may well choke off a tree's breathing. For this reason it will be necessary to build a "well" around your tree.

If you need to raise the level of the grade, pile rocks and crushed stone immediately around the tree. But do not place the rocks and stone where it will make contact with the trunk. Use tile pipes as vents (and as feeding tubes). This will permit air to reach the area of the natural ground level and permit continued aeration of the soil around the root zone. Figure 23 illustrates how this is done. In building a well, it should be recognized that good drainage is essential, too, since the collection of water in the system could drown the roots, and cause the tree to die.

In lowering the level of the grade, the original soil must be retained and not disturbed. Grade around the periphery of the tree and build a stone wall, as shown in the diagram.

How to Save Structurally Weak Trees

Besides insects and disease, natural conditions are sometimes responsible for structurally weakened trees or structurally weakened parts of trees. Weakening occurs when a tree is cracked by frost, split by lightning, or damaged severely by an ice storm. A tree with a large cavity in its trunk is almost certain to be weak and subject to damage by strong wind gusts. A tree with a double leader (Y-shaped) is likely to split into two parts at its crotch as the limbs grow larger and become heavier. A leaning tree or one on an eroding slope faces the danger of toppling.

To complicate problems further, a tree with a split or cavity is exposed to additional damage by insects, disease, and decay.

When your trees are weakened in any of these ways, artificial supports, as well as tree surgery, are necessary. Judicious efforts now will save you money and added trouble in the long run. Most of the work required to overcome these problems involves either *cable bracing* or *bolt bracing*. These tasks may appear to be very simple and sometimes unnecessary. Actually, they are difficult and exacting processes.

ᏀᎦ CABLE BRACING—FOR STRENGTHENING WEAK CROTCHES. Flexible cable may be used in bracing trees in order to strengthen weak

Figure 23

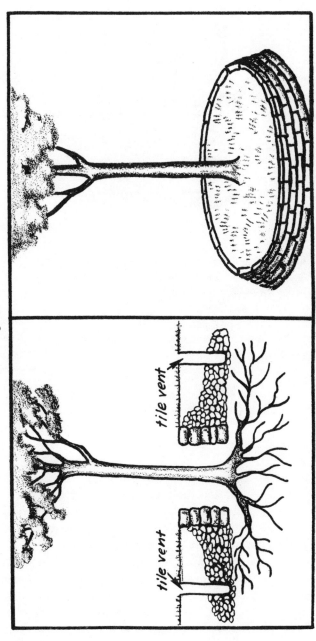

WHEN THE GRADE IS RAISED

When adding soil over the root zone is necessary, pile rocks around the trunk as shown. Then add crushed stone and gravel. Include in your plan about eight tile vents for circulation of air and for feeding. The vents may be ordinary pipes.

WHEN THE GRADE IS LOWERED

When removing soil from around the tree, avoid disturbing the soil over the root system. Retain original soil by building wall around the root zone, as shown above.

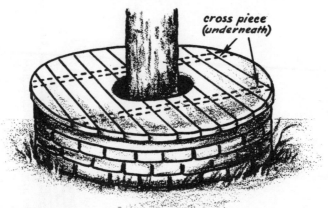

Figure 24

The homeowner with imagination can make use of a tree well in his yard. One idea is a garden bench either for sitting or for the placement of outdoor plants.

crotches, to brace trees together, or to support a transplanted tree until the root system is established.

ঔ CABLING. As a general rule, cables should be placed as high in the tree as practicable when it is necessary to prevent a weak crotch from splitting. If placed about two thirds of the distance from crotch to branch tips, this takes maximum advantage of the law of lever and fulcrum.

The supplies needed for this work include lag screws, eyebolts, thimbles, and seven-wire strand cable (see Figure 25). Cable comes in various diameters—such as ⅛″, ¼″, ⅜″, ⅝″—and should be chosen according to the weight it must support. What precisely you will need depends, of course, on the nature of your problem.

In deciding where to place cables, several factors must be kept in mind. Cables should not be placed where they will rub against limbs and cause abrasions. Screws are as satisfactory as bolts in bracing the branches of hardwood trees. However, eyebolts are safer for use in bracing softwoods or hardwoods having some decay. If it is necessary to install a lag screw or eyebolt near the crotch, it

Figure 25

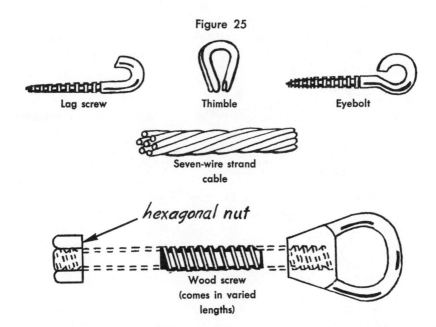

is advisable to stay from six to twelve inches above or below the crotch. The cable should be placed so that the cable anchors (lags or bolts) on each limb are equidistant from the crotch.

Once it is determined where to place the cables, you will have to decide whether a single cable is strong enough to brace two large, heavy limbs. This may not be a simple decision; the installation of at least one additional cable may be necessary. However, experience has shown that placing a cable two thirds of the distance from the crotch to the end of the tree limbs is usually adequate.

The first step in cable bracing is to drill holes in the limbs at the points where the lags will be inserted. The holes should be one sixteenth of an inch smaller in diameter than the lag. They should be drilled slightly deeper than the length of the lag thread so as to prevent splitting. In doing so, remember that the cable and lag will need to form a straight line at the point of attachment. Lags should be screwed in to a point that will just allow slipping the cable splices over the hooks.

After the lags are inserted, the limbs may be drawn together slightly by means of a rope slung between the limbs and tightened by twisting. This is done to prevent slack in the cable, which is certain to appear after the cable has had a chance to stretch.[1] Slack must not be given the chance to develop. Doing this in advance will enable you to measure the length of cable you will need. (See Figure 26.)

A cable may be attached to a lag by means of an eye splice. (See Figure 27.)

If eyebolts are used instead of lags, the procedure is the same except for the drilling of holes. They should be the same diameter as the bolts; it will be necessary to provide a countersink for the nut and washer. (See Figure 28.)

ॐ OTHER TYPES OF CABLE BRACING. If you have a leaning tree that is likely to topple someday, you may wish to cable it to a nearby tree for support. In such an instance, the same procedures for attaching the cable apply.

To support a transplanted tree with cabling in guy-wire fashion, see Figure 5.

ॐ BOLT BRACING—FOR REPAIRING SPLITS. Bolt bracing involves the use of wood screws to repair splits in the trunks of trees. (See Figure 29.) Wood screws come in prepared lengths and various diameters. They are threaded and are used with nuts and washers. (See Figure 25.)

To "sew up" a long split in a limb or trunk, it will first be necessary to clean and treat the wound, using techniques described in Figure 12. Then, through both sides of the split, drill holes of the same diameter as the wood screw. Where the nuts and washers are placed, cut out countersinks. (See Figure 28.) If more than one wood screw is needed, space them twelve to sixteen inches apart.

When tightening the nuts in order to close up the split, care must be exercised to prevent injury to the bark and cambium.

Repairing a Trunk Cavity

One of the authors recalls that years ago an acquaintance repaired the hole in a tree by simply filling it with concrete cement—nothing else. But his efforts were in vain. The cement shrank just enough to

[1] Tests indicate that a seven-strand cable will stretch at least an inch per foot of length.

Figure 26

The double leader of a tree properly cable-braced to prevent a split at the crotch.

Figure 27

STEPS IN MAKING AN EYE SPLICE IN SEVEN-WIRE STRAND

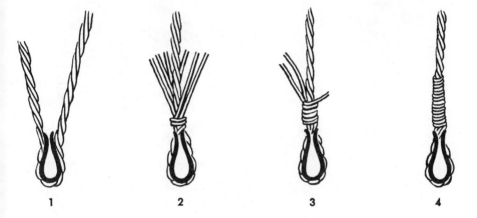

1   2   3   4

This shows how to make an eye splice for attaching a cable to a lag screw or eyebolt. First, a loop is made by bending the cable about 10″ to 12″ from the end; then a thimble, or eye, is inserted in the loop. The wires of the 10″ section are then unwrapped and laid along parallel to the main piece of cable. One strand is selected, and wrapped with pliers tightly around both the cable and the remaining six strands. Two wraps are made with this strand, which is then cut off. The rest of the strands are then wrapped one at a time, as with the first strand.

Figure 28

front view

A countersink is provided whenever nuts and washers are used. To prepare, the exact shape of the washer (round, oval, or diamond) is first marked with a chisel on the bark. Then this bark and about ⅛" of wood are cut out and removed. The cambium edge should then be shellacked. The back of the countersink must be exactly at right angles to the direction of the bolt so that the washer may lie perfectly flat. This procedure will enable the wound to heal properly.

side view

Figure 29

(Looking downward) A split "sewed up" with a wood screw

allow moisture to seep in. Internal decay resulted and went unnoticed until the tree had to be chopped down in later years.

The correct way to repair a cavity is first to clean it thoroughly, using a knife or chisel to remove all signs of decay inside the hole. Then spray inside of hole with an insecticide or fungicide to disinfect. Next, a certain amount of bolt bracing may be necessary to replace artificially the inherent strength of the decayed or removed woody tissue and to hold the cavity walls in position. How much bolt bracing will depend upon the size of the cavity.

Following the instructions for bolt bracing above, use wood screws for internal cross bracing. This involves alternate placement of wood-screw rods diagonally across the deep cavity to form an X shape. (See Figure 30.) Such bracing will keep the sidewalls from spreading, and will tend to minimize the twisting strains that do so much damage to filling materials.

Cavities are no longer filled as they used to be. Instead, they are thoroughly cleaned out to remove all decay, treated for insects and disease, and supported if necessary. It's important that the cavity walls be exposed to air so they can be treated periodically, as needed. (See Figure 12.)

Figure 30

(Looking downward) Wood-screw rods should cross in X fashion to provide adequate support against splitting.

Equipping a Tree with Lightning Protection

Trees that are most likely to be struck and damaged by lightning include oaks, hickories, elms, sycamores, spruces, and tall trees in moist or wet areas. While there is a slim chance that your trees—if among these—will ever be hit by lightning, you may want to ensure against this possibility. Particularly because the hazards and consequences are so great when a tree in your yard is struck, you will want to consider very carefully the installation of lightning protection.

Trees that especially need protection are those higher than your home. Where there is a group of trees, only a few of the tallest need to be protected.

Lightning protection may be rather expensive. It can be accomplished by using one or more air terminals, copper rods or tubes of varied lengths at least five eighths of an inch thick. They are placed at the highest secure branches of the tree. They must be grounded through a conductor, which is a part of the system connecting the air terminals with the grounds. A good conductor is made of aluminum or copper three eighths of an inch thick. Very large trees may need two conductors and several air terminals. All systems should be grounded with at least two ground connections. (See Figure 31.)

Mount the conductor line with long-shanked screw fasteners (see Figure 32) to keep the conductors from being in contact with the tree when a lightning discharge is carried through the system.

To make a ground connection, dig a trench and bury the unraveled end of the conductor cable in it. Make the trench shallow near the tree to prevent damage to the roots. Make it slant downward, away from the base of the tree, so as to reach moist soil if possible.

Unfortunately, the average person has neither the equipment nor the skill to install and test correctly a lightning-protection system. And for this reason, the one who is not sure of himself should hire a tree specialist for the work. In any event, materials approved by Underwriters Laboratories, Inc. should be used. All such materials are clearly labeled.

Make a periodic inspection of your lightning-protection system to be sure it will be able to serve you at the crucial moment. Look for bent, loose, or missing air terminals, broken conductor cables, and loose long-shanked screw fasteners when you inspect.

DO's and DON'T's

Cable and Bolt Bracing

Don't cable too tightly, but do allow for stretching. (Consider the freedom of movement a limb needs when the wind blows.)

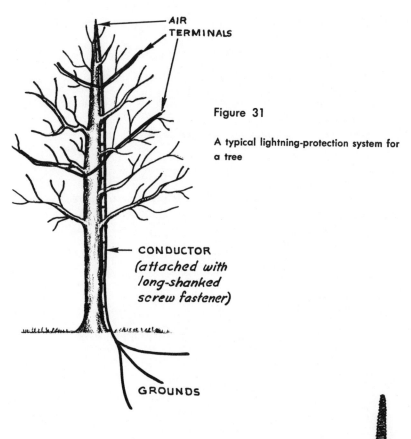

AIR
TERMINALS

Figure 31

A typical lightning-protection system for
a tree

CONDUCTOR
*(attached with
long-shanked
screw fastener)*

GROUNDS

Figure 32

Long-shanked screw fastener used for
mounting a conductor cable to tree

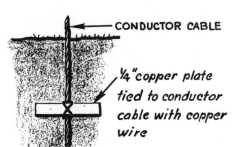

CONDUCTOR CABLE

*¼"copper plate
tied to conductor
cable with copper
wire*

Figure 33

Ground made by burying a plate of
sheet copper

Don't drill holes into limbs that are very small.

When closing up a split, install one additional wood-screw brace at the fork to ensure against further splitting.

After bracing, heavy root feeding with a tree food will help speed the repair of tree splits and other tree injuries.

Never permit cables to be wrapped around trunks or branches for anchorage. (In time, they will cause serious damage.)

After a wood-screw brace is in place, it is important that the end of the rod be rounded off with a ball peen hammer to prevent the nut from working loose.

In bolt bracing, care should be taken that consecutive holes are not in the same direct line of sap flow, but are staggered.

Cables should be placed where they will not rub against limbs and cause abrasions.

Only one cable should be attached to each lag, and lags should be at least twelve inches apart.

Miscellaneous

In welling a tree when the grade is lowered, don't pile rocks so that they touch the trunk, and thereby cause decay.

Septic systems above tree roots are good for trees as long as the roots do not grow into them. Be sure your septic system has continuous bacteria action. It's good tree food.

When installing lightning protection, lead the conductor toward the ground away from the house.

Remove brush beneath trees by hand. If you want to add a bit of topsoil, turn it over or level it off. Use a shovel, *not* a bulldozer.

Examine your trees periodically for structural weaknesses.

Safety Tips

Wear gloves and proper clothing when working in a tree.

Beware of poison ivy.

Be sure children and others keep a safe distance when you're doing your work.

Get help in lifting heavy objects. But, if you must lift, use your leg muscles—*not* your back muscles.

Be sure the ladder you use is not broken, and is secure before you climb it.

Never leave tools in trees.

Avoid working near charged wires.

Be careful in handling and using sharp tools and materials.

Use a safety belt when working in a tree.

8 GETTING THE HELP OF A TREE EXPERT

What a Tree Expert Can Do for You

This book has attempted to explain what the homeowner himself can do to care for his trees. It may appear that growing trees is a gigantic task, and perhaps not worth the trouble. It *can* be a big job, but be assured it is well worth the trouble—if you want trees. However, with minimum time to care for his trees, the average person is likely to take the quickest shortcut to solve his problems, and neglect those that appear unimportant at the moment.

For the tree gardener who wants to give his trees the best of care, but does not have the time or requires professional guidance, there is always the tree expert. He is a tree specialist who can advise someone who is about to build what trees are worth saving or who can advise an established homeowner concerning any problems he may have with his trees, and recommend curative or preventive measures. He has the knowledge that enables him to diagnose tree ills, and he is equipped with tools and machinery that are essential for tree work most average homeowners would be physically unable to carry out. He has the skill and know-how, backed by experience and, generally, the proper training. Together, the tree expert and tree owner must work hand in hand, not necessarily physically, but cooperatively. The object, of course, is to keep your trees alive, growing, healthy, and beautiful.

A trained tree expert is equipped to do in minutes a job that probably would take you hours. He does it without muss or fuss, and you're satisfied because you respect his expertise. In addition, his services save you time for other tasks.

You Need a Professional Tree Expert

- when you don't have time to do the work
- when the trees are too large for you to handle or when you're physically unable to do the work
- when the technical procedures are too complicated to understand
- when a professional diagnosis is essential
- when you don't own or have access to the necessary equipment and tools
- when you want to be certain about a diagnosis and the necessary remedial steps
- when you're planning to build where there are existing trees
- when special licensing is needed for chemical application

How to Choose a Tree Expert

Unfortunately, getting a qualified expert isn't simple, unless you deal with a reputable tree firm operating in your area.

Don't choose just anybody! It's always good to learn through your friends and neighbors who has done a competent, successful, economical job for them. Though an unknown *may* work out to your satisfaction, you're running a big risk. But if you do decide to hire an unknown professional tree man to do your work, ask pointed questions to test his reliability before you come to an agreement. This is one way the knowledge derived from this book will prove fruitful.

Try to determine whether he is conscientious, businesslike, and steady. Does he have the proper equipment and tools to do the job? What is his background or experience? Are his methods of working safe? Does he carry insurance; if not, are *you* properly covered for all eventualities? In talking to him, try to decide whether he is sincerely interested in the welfare of your trees more than he is interested in earning a living or getting the job over with.

Unfortunate incidents involving poor workmanship by men calling themselves "tree experts" do occur. Here are two examples. In one case, the wrong method was employed in cutting down a tree. The result? A crushed cabin. In the other case, the tree man sprayed the foliage of a tree with unnecessarily high pressure, causing the tree to lose all its leaves shortly afterward. These examples serve to illustrate why it is important to hire someone who is a bona fide tree expert.

What Will His Services Cost?

There's not much point in discussing estimates with a tree man if you don't feel he will do the job properly. When he visits you to discuss the problem, your primary concern is your trees. Don't allow a low "come-on" price to bias your thinking. But after you are positively sold on him, and you both have agreed what has to be done, it is important to discuss the terms before he begins his work. If you wish, you may want to consider calling in another tree man to "price-shop."

In any event, professional tree men charge by the hour, or they may charge a flat sum based on an itemized contract. Sometimes the price is figured on the basis of an annual maintenance plan. There are no established prices that all tree experts follow as a rule of thumb. The price usually depends on precisely what has to be done. Sometimes, by having two or three neighboring families contract to have their trees sprayed during the tree man's one visit, everybody can save money.

Operation "Payoff"

The estimate for treating a tree may at first appear to be out of line with your pocketbook or budget, but do try to think about what would happen if you should lose that tree merely by doing nothing about it. Consider two actual experiences that, fortunately, turned out happily.

In one instance, a retired couple living in a Cleveland suburb noticed that the pin oak in their front yard, which was forty to fifty years old, was losing its leaves during the summer months. Sensing a serious problem, they immediately called in an expert local tree firm to determine the trouble and what could be done to save the tree.

They were told that the tree would require special treatment, including a feeding, and that the cost would be $240. If the couple had hesitated to take action immediately, the tree might have died. Their temporary saving of $240 would have resulted in a bill totaling more than that amount just to remove a dead tree that, as long as it stood, endangered life and property.

Just outside New York City, a big Norway spruce had developed a large, unsightly cavity that had begun a few years earlier with an open wound in the trunk. The owner finally called in a tree expert, who suggested that the cavity be cleaned and filled at a cost of $385. The owner agreed. Had he continued to postpone attention to the problem, the heartwood eventually would have rotted to such a degree that a windstorm might easily have toppled the tree. The longer he procrastinated, the more local life and property were jeopardized, not to mention nearby power lines. Removal of the tree was estimated at $425.

These are typical of experiences, involving the services of trained professional tree men everywhere, where tree owners hired experts not only to save their trees but also to retain what may have taken a generation or a lifetime to obtain: shade, beauty, and the benefits to property and the environment that such magnificent trees bring.

We, as amateur tree experts, have a big job periodically inspecting the trees on our grounds and doing what we can do to prevent small problems from becoming large and expensive ones. But if and when the real trouble comes, and it is something you can't undertake yourself, don't underestimate the help the professional tree expert can give you. You owe it to your trees and to yourself.

CHARTS

CHART A

STANDARDS FOR NURSERY-GROWN TREES*
(as recommended by the American Association of Nurserymen, Inc.)

MOST STANDARD SHADE TREES

If the caliber[1] is	the suggested height[2] is	minimum root spread if bare-rooted	minimum diameter of rootball if balled and burlapped
½" to ¾"	5' to 6'	12"	n/s[3]
¾" to 1"	6' to 8'	16"	n/s
1" to 1¼"	7' to 9'	18"	n/s
1¼" to 1½"	8' to 10'	20"	18"
1½" to 1¾"	10' to 12'	22"	20"
1¾" to 2"	10' to 12'	24"	22"
2" to 2½"	12' to 14'	28"	24"
2½" to 3"	12' to 14'	32"	28"
3" to 3½"	14' to 16'	38"	32"

* From "American Standard for Nursery Stock," Z60.1—1959, sponsored by the American Association of Nurserymen, Inc., approved by the United States of America Standards Institute. Subject to periodic review and revision.

[1] To determine the caliber of a tree, measure the diameter of the trunk at a point 6" above ground level. (For trees with a caliber of more than 4", measure diameter at a point 12" above ground level.)

[2] Minimum heights. The height of a tree does not include the roots or that portion of the tree that is below ground level when planted.

[3] n/s—No standard listed.

MOST SMALL ORNAMENTAL TREES (except evergreens)

If the height is	the minimum diameter of rootball should be
1½' to 2'	10"
2' to 3'	12"
3' to 4'	13"
4' to 5'	15"
5' to 6'	16"
6' to 7'	18"
7' to 8'	20"
8' to 9'	22"
9' to 10'	24"
10' to 12'	26"

FRUIT TREES

	CALIBER			
	$11/16''-1''$	$9/16''-11/16''$	$7/16''-9/16''$	$5/16''-7/16''$
apple: standard	4½' +	4' +	3' +	2' +
apple: dwarf		3½' +	2½' +	2' +
apricot	4' +	3' +	2½' +	2' +
cherry: sour (one year)	3½' +	3' +	2½' +	2' +
cherry: sweet	4½' +	4' +	3' +	2' +
peach	4½' +	4' +	3' +	2' +
pear: standard	4½' +	4' +	3' +	2' +
pear: dwarf		3½' +	3' +	2' +
plum	4½' +	4' +	3' +	2' +
quince		3½' +	3' +	2' +

CHART B

TREES BY SIZE AT MATURITY

(In some locations this table may not prove 100 percent accurate, since the rate of tree growth varies in different climates and soils.)

small to medium trees (to 50' in height)

Breadth: 25'–30' or Less

Apple, Crab
Arborvitae
Aspen
Birch, Clump
Cedar, Red
Cherry, Flowering
Dogwood, Flowering
Dogwood, Pacific
Elm, Slippery
Elm, Winged
Evergreen Privet
Fruit Trees, most
Golden Chain
Greenwattle Acacia
Hackberry
Hawthorn
Holly, American
Holly, English
Judas Tree
Locust, Black

Locust, Moraine
Maple, Japanese
Mimosa
Mountain Ash
Mulberry
Palmetto, Cabbage
Pine, Austrian
Pine, Red
Pine, Scotch
Oak, Blackjack
Redbud
Sassafras
Serviceberry
Shadbush
Silk Tree
Sweet Bay
Sweet Gum
Yellowwood
Yew (all varieties)

medium to large trees (50'–100' height or more)

Breadth: 25'–30' or Less

Cottonwood
Ginkgo
Hickory, Shagbark
Oak, Pin
Oak, Post
Palm, Washington
Pecan

Persimmon
Pine, Lodgepole
Pine, Short-Leaf
Poplar
Spruce
Sugarberry

medium to large trees (50'–100' height or more)

Breadth: 30' or More

Ailanthus
Ash (except Mountain Ash)
Basswood, American (Linden)
Beech
Birch, Black
Birch, Canoe
Birch, European White
Birch, Paper
Birch, Red
Birch, River
Birch, Yellow
Bitternut
Black Gum
Box Elder
Buttonball
Catalpa
Cherry, Black
Chestnut
Cucumber Tree Magnolia
Elm, American
Elm, English
Fir, Balsam
Fir, California Red
Fir, Douglas
Hemlock
Hickory, Swamp
Horse Chestnut
Larch (Tamarack)
Linden (American Basswood)
Locust, Honey
Locust, Thorny
Magnolia, Cucumber Tree
Magnolia, Southern
Maple, Big Leaf
Maple, Black

Maple, Norway
Maple, Red
Maple, Schwedler's
Maple, Silver
Maple, Sugar
Maple, Swamp
Oak, Black (Rock)
Oak, Bur
Oak, California White
Oak, Chestnut
Oak, Northern Red
Oak, Scarlet
Oak, Southern Red
Oak, Spanish
Oak, Swamp Chestnut
Oak, Swamp Red
Oak, Swamp White
Oak, Water
Oak, White
Oak, Willow
Oak, Yellow
Pepperidge
Pine, Ponderosa
Pine, Sugar
Pine, White
Plane, American
Plane, London
Sour Gum
Sycamore, American (Plane)
Tamarack
Tulip (Yellow Poplar)
Tupelo, Black
Walnut, Black
Willow

CHART C
RATE OF GROWTH OF TREES

faster-growing trees

Ailanthus
Apple, Crab
Ash, Black
Ash, Green
Ash, Red
Aspen
Basswood, American (Linden)
Black Gum
Buttonball
Catalpa
Cherry, Flowering
Cottonwood
Cucumber Tree Magnolia
Elm, Slippery
Evergreen Privet
Fir, Balsam
Fir, California Red
Fir, Douglas
Golden Chain
Greenwattle Acacia
Hemlock
Linden (American Basswood)
Locust, Moraine
Magnolia, Cucumber Tree
Magnolia, Southern
Maple, Japanese

Maple, Norway
Maple, Red
Maple, Schwedler's
Maple, Silver
Maple, Swamp
Mimosa
Mountain Ash
Oak, Pin
Oak, Scarlet
Oak, Water
Oak, Willow
Pepperidge
Pine, White
Plane, American
Poplar
Sassafras
Serviceberry
Silk Tree
Sour Gum
Sycamore, American (Plane)
Tulip (Yellow Poplar)
Tupelo, Black
    (Black Gum, Sour Gum)
Willow
Yew (all varieties)

slower-growing trees

Arborvitae
Ash, White
Beech
Birch (all varieties)
Bitternut
Box Elder
Cedar, Red
Cherry
Chestnut

Dogwood, Flowering
Dogwood, Pacific
Elm, American
Elm, English
Elm, Winged
Ginkgo
Hackberry
Hawthorn
Hickory

Holly, American
Holly, English
Horse Chestnut
Judas Tree
Larch (Tamarack)
Locust, Black
Locust, Honey
Locust, Thorny
Maple, Big Leaf
Maple, Black
Maple, Sugar
Mulberry, Red
Oak, Black (Rock)
Oak, Blackjack
Oak, Bur
Oak, California White
Oak, Chestnut
Oak, Northern Red
Oak, Post
Oak, Southern Red
Oak, Spanish
Oak, Swamp Chestnut
Oak, Swamp Red
Oak, Swamp White

Oak, White
Oak, Yellow
Palm, Washington
Palmetto, Cabbage
Pecan
Persimmon
Pine, Austrian
Pine, Lodgepole
Pine, Ponderosa
Pine, Red
Pine, Scotch
Pine, Short-Leaf
Pine, Sugar
Plane, London
Redbud
Shadbush
Spruce
Sugarberry
Sweet Bay
Sweet Gum
Tamarack
Walnut, Black
Yellowwood

CHART D
APPROXIMATE BEARING AGES OF FRUIT TREES*
(from planting time)

	years
apple	4 to 7
apricot	4 to 5
sour cherry	4 to 5
sweet cherry	5 to 7
citrus	3 to 5
fig	2 to 3
peach	3 to 4
pear	4 to 6
plum	4 to 6
quince	5 to 6

* Source: United States Department of Agriculture.

CHART E

HOW TO IMPROVE INFERIOR SOILS

if your soil is	do this
Sandy	Cultivate and work in small amounts of any fertilizer high in phosphorus and potassium content. If a commercial fertilizer is used, small quantities of manure must also be added. Refertilize periodically.
Clayey	Cultivate and turn over the soil as much as possible, at the same time adding sand and humus to improve aeration and drainage.

CHART F

TREES HAVE THEIR PREFERENCES: SWEET OR SOUR SOIL

acid (sour) about pH_5

Ailanthus	Laurel, Mountain	Quince
Aspen	Magnolia	Serviceberry
Birch	Mountain Ash	Shadbush
Cottonwood	Oak, Pin	Spruce
Fir	Orange	Sugarberry
Hemlock	Pecan	Willow
Holly	Persimmon, Common	
Larch	Pine	

slightly acid about pH_6 or pH_7

Apricot	Cedar, Red and White	Greenwattle Acacia
Black Gum	Chestnut	Hackberry
Box Elder	Cypress	Hawthorn
Catalpa	Ginkgo	Hickory

Judas Tree
Maples
Oak, Black
Oak, Blackjack
Oak, Bur
Oak, Chestnut
Oak, Northern Red
Oak, Post
Oak, Red

Oak, Scarlet
Oak, Scrub
Oak, Southern Red
Oak, Spanish
Oak, Swamp Chestnut
Oak, Swamp Red
Oak, Swamp White
Oak, Water
Oak, Willow

Oak, Yellow
Pepperidge
Redbud
Sassafras
Sour Gum
Sweet Bay
Tupelo, Black
Yellowwood

slightly alkaline (sweet) pH_7–pH_8 range

Apple
Ash, Black, Green,
    Red, or White
Beech
Buttonball
Cherry
Dogwood
Elm, American, Slip-
    pery, or Winged
Horse Chestnut

Juniper
Lilac
Linden
Locust
Mimosa
Mulberry
Oak, White
Palm, Washington
Palmetto, Cabbage
Peach

Pear
Plane
Plum
Poplar
Silk Tree
Sweet Gum
Sycamore
Tulip Tree
Walnut
Yew

CHART G

SEASONAL GUIDE FOR PRUNING

JANUARY
FEBRUARY
MARCH

1. Prune shade trees and fruit trees, removing deadwood and interfering branches. Shape fruit trees for
   support as well as for production.
2. Now is a good time to remove dead or undesirable
   trees, with as little damage as possible to lawns and
   gardens.

APRIL
MAY
JUNE

1. Prune flowering trees and shrubs as soon as possible
   after blooming so as to preserve the blossoms for
   next year.
2. Thin out fruit where two are touching, to eliminate
   their collecting moisture at the point of contact, causing possible rot.

JULY   1. Prune evergreens and hedges now, to allow them to
AUGUST   develop new growth for winter protection.
SEPTEMBER   2. Thin shade trees by pruning away interfering branches.
               Do vista work now while leaves are still alive.

OCTOBER   1. As leaves just begin to change color, prune out weak
NOVEMBER   branches that have a premature leaf fall to prevent
DECEMBER   their showing up as dead branches next spring.
            2. With burlap, cover delicate evergreens and other
               specimens that will be exposed to wintry blasts.

CHART H
WHO'S WHO AMONG THE BUGS[1]

beneficial	attacks and feeds on . . .
ant lion	(traps insects in a hole)
bald-faced hornet	caterpillars
bee fly	larvae of other insects
black wasp	Japanese beetles
Tiphia popilliavora	
caterpillar hunter	gypsy moths, tent caterpillars
cicada killer	locusts
click beetle	insects
cornfield ant	aphid secretions
dragonfly	small insects
earwigs (some varieties)	various insect pests
lacewing	aphids, etc.
ladybug	aphids and insects
lightning bug	young aphids and aphid eggs
mud wasp	caterpillars and beetle larvae
praying mantis	various insect pests
rove beetles	scavengers and insects
syrphus fly	aphids and scales
tachinid	larvae of insects
tiger beetle	insects

[1] Many of these beneficial insects are available to the homeowner. Call the county agricultural agent in your locality for information.

CHART I

DIAGNOSIS AND PREVENTION OF COMMON TREE INSECT AND DISEASE PROBLEMS

Symptoms	Kinds of Trees Affected	Probable Trouble	Suggested Treatment
FOLIAGE TORN OR PUNCTURED			
holes and tears in leaves (in spring)	most shade and flowering trees	cankerworms	Spray foliage with stomach or contact poison as recommended on pages 77–79. Band trunk per instructions on page 84 to prevent invasion of additional cankerworms.
leaves almost completely devoured (in summer months)	many varieties of shade and ornamental trees	gypsy moth caterpillars	Spray foliage with stomach or contact poison, or fumigant, as recommended on pages 77–79; band tree trunk per instructions on page 84 to prevent invasion of additional gypsy moth caterpillars.
holes in leaves (after July 1)	fruit, shade, ornamental trees less than 25 feet in height	Japanese beetles	Pick beetles off by hand and drop them in open jar of kerosene. Spray tree with stomach or contact poison, or fumigant, as recommended on pages 77–79.

Symptoms	Kinds of Trees Affected	Probable Trouble	Suggested Treatment
eaten foliage	sassafras and magnolias	sassafras weevils	Spray foliage with contact poison or fumigant as recommended on pages 77–79.
eaten foliage	black walnut and hickory trees	walnut caterpillars	Spray foliage with stomach or contact poison as recommended on pages 77–79.
eaten foliage	larch tree and most conifers, including pines and spruces	larch sawflies	Spray foliage with stomach or contact poison as recommended on pages 77–79.
holes in leaves; defoliation of leaves	elms	elm leaf beetles	Spray foliage with stomach or contact poison as recommended on pages 77–79.
leaves and new shoots eaten	evergreen privet	privet web worms	Prune away affected parts and spray foliage with contact poison or fumigant as recommended on pages 77–79.
leaves and new shoots eaten	poplar and cotton-wood trees	cottonwood leaf beetles	Spray foliage with stomach or contact poison as recommended on pages 77–79.
leaves and new shoots eaten	willows, elms, poplars	willow worms	Spray foliage with stomach or contact poison as recommended on pages 77–79.

Symptoms	Kinds of Trees Affected	Probable Trouble	Suggested Treatment
edges of leaves eaten (usually discovered in morning but not noticed day before)	rhododendrons and other broad leaf plantings	snails	Broadcast treated pellets (available at garden shops) under broad leaf evergreens.
leaves eaten; small, weblike bags hanging from branches	evergreens and deciduous trees	bag worms	Hand-pick the bags. Spray foliage with contact poison or fumigant as recommended on pages 77–79.
buds eaten and evidence of leaf chewing	fruit and small shade and ornamental trees	ant worms	Spray foliage with stomach or contact poison as recommended on pages 77–79.
buds and underside of foliage eaten away	pecan trees	bud moths	Spray foliage with stomach or contact poison as recommended on pages 77–79.

FOLIAGE WITH VISIBLE INSECTS

leaves covered with tent caterpillars	fruit trees and sometimes deciduous trees	tent caterpillars eating foliage	Spray with stomach or contact poison, or fumigant, as recommended on pages 77–79; band tree trunk per instructions on page 84 to prevent invasion of additional tent caterpillars.

Symptoms	Kinds of Trees Affected	Probable Trouble	Suggested Treatment
curled leaf enclosing green worm with black head (before July 1)	most shade and flowering trees	leaf rollers	Spray foliage with contact poison or fumigant as recommended on pages 77–79.

FOLIAGE DISCOLORED OR SPOTTED

Symptoms	Kinds of Trees Affected	Probable Trouble	Suggested Treatment
brown spots on leaves	catalpa trees	various fungi	In fall gather fallen leaves and burn them (check local ordinances). In early spring spray new foliage with fungicide as recommended on pages 77–79.
pale green or brown spots on leaves	yellow poplars (tulip tree)	tulip-tree aphids	Spray foliage with contact poison or fumigant as recommended on pages 77–79.
bottom surfaces of leaves turn brown	apple tree	apple bucculatrix	Spray foliage with a fungicide as recommended on pages 77–79.
bottom side of leaves turn brown	most deciduous trees, rhododendrons, andromedas, and azaleas	lace bugs	Spray foliage with contact poison as recommended on pages 77–79.
light color or brown spots on bottom side of leaves	honey or moraine locust trees	honey locust mite	Spray foliage with a contact poison or fumigant as recommended on pages 77–79.
irregular, brownish blisters on leaves	shade and fruit trees	leaf blister mites	Spray foliage, using a dormant oil with ethion.

Symptoms	Kinds of Trees Affected	Probable Trouble	Suggested Treatment
leaves turn brown, tear, and shred	birch, oak, and elm trees	an infection caused by leaf miners	Spray foliage in April or early May with a fumigant as recommended on pages 77–79.
brown patches in leaf fibers; also early leaf fall	elms	elm sawfly leaf miners	Spray foliage with a fumigant as recommended on pages 77–79.
small to large light-brown, purple, or black spots or dead areas on leaves, sometimes merging; whole leaf tends to be disfigured; finally dies	plane, maple, sycamore, oak, and hickory trees	anthracnose (a fungus)	Spray 2 or 3 times with a recommended fungicide (see pages 77–79) at 7- to 10-day intervals, starting with the first leaf development early the following spring.
spots on leaves; usually small, irregularly circular, and reddish brown with purplish borders	maple trees	leaf spot (a fungus)	Spray 2 or 3 times with a recommended fungicide (see pages 77–79) at 7- to 10-day intervals, starting with the first leaf development early the following spring.
tiny growths (swellings) on leaves; green at first, then turning red	maple trees	maple leaf gall (a microscopic mite)	Spray with malathion in early spring after leaves bud, and twice again as the leaves develop to their normal matured size.

Symptoms	Kinds of Trees Affected	Probable Trouble	Suggested Treatment
margins of leaves or tissues between leaf veins turn brown	sugar and Norway maples	leaf scorch	Feed and water tree. Maintain routine control of insect pests that threaten the tree's health.
swift browning of leaves followed by dieback of one limb after another	red oaks	oak wilt (a fungus)	Contact a tree professional.
bright yellow leaves on certain high branches (in July and August); also brown discoloration of inner bark of branches	American elm trees	Dutch elm disease (a fungus)	Cut off affected parts. Feed tree well in early spring and late fall. Spray with a combination of Sevin and methoxychlor or a combination of Sevin and metacytox. Call a tree specialist.
leaves wilt, dry, and drop in mid- or late summer; green streaks appear in leaf stems, twigs, and branches	Norway, sugar, red, silver, Japanese, big-leaf, box elder, hedge and sycamore maples and ailanthus trees	maple wilt (a fungus)	Prune away all dead or dying twigs and branches. Water tree well during droughts. Aerate root zone. Feed in fall. A special tree injection may be necessary. Call a tree expert.
notches in edges of leaves and needles	yews, hemlocks, mountain laurels, ilex, rhododendrons	taxus weevils, slugs or snails (may also be feeding on roots)	Spray tree with malathion and treat soil with a chemical pellet for snails and slugs, available at garden shops.

Symptoms	Kinds of Trees Affected	Probable Trouble	Suggested Treatment
water-soaked spots develop on leaves, followed by the appearance of small dark spots on the top surface of leaves between veins.	maple trees	tar spots (a fungus)	With a recommended fungicide (see pages 77–79), spray when leafbuds are opening early the following spring. Spray 2 or 3 times (10 to 20 days apart) if spring is a wet one.

FOLIAGE LOSS

Symptoms	Kinds of Trees Affected	Probable Trouble	Suggested Treatment
massive defoliation of uppermost part of tree	all trees	lack of food, water, and/or air in root zone	Punch holes in ground under tree to aerate root zone. Feed and water tree in root zone.
discoloration of foliage, followed by leaf drop beginning on lower limbs	dogwoods	fungus disease	Spray foliage in early May with Benlate, and again in mid-May. Consult a tree specialist.
defoliation of branches; holes in other leaves	elms	elm leaf beetles	Spray foliage with a contact or stomach poison as recommended on pages 77–79.

TRUNKS AND LIMBS WITH DISEASED GROWTHS

Symptoms	Kinds of Trees Affected	Probable Trouble	Suggested Treatment
brownish-purple, cotton-like mass (oyster-shaped)	orange and lemon trees	purple scale (an insect)	Spray foliage with a fumigant as recommended on pages 77–79.

Symptoms	Kinds of Trees Affected	Probable Trouble	Suggested Treatment
yellowish or reddish, cottonlike mass (circular-shaped)	citrus fruit trees	red scale (an insect)	Spray foliage with a fumigant as recommended on pages 77–79.
large, soft, dark brown to black cotton-like mass	citrus fruit trees	black scale (an insect)	Spray foliage with a fumigant as recommended on pages 77–79.
cottony, scaly substance	elms, junipers, pines, magnolias, poplars, sycamores, oaks, hemlocks	scale insect	Spray with miscible oil in very early spring. Follow up with contact poison as recommended on pages 77–79.
localized diseased area of bark (like a large sore)	maples and oaks	canker disease (trunk is weakened considerably if not checked when disease is young)	Call in a tree specialist to prune out and treat affected areas.
pinhead-sized, circular, crusty growth on branches; also small red spots on fruit	mostly fruit and some shade and evergreen trees	San Jose scale (an insect)	Spray branches with miscible oil in early spring. Follow up with a contact poison as recommended on pages 77–79.
white, waxy masses in base of needle clusters, and on sprouts and branches	fruit trees, evergreens, shade, and ornamental trees	woolly aphids (an insect)	Spray with a fumigant as recommended on pages 77–79.

Symptoms	Kinds of Trees Affected	Probable Trouble	Suggested Treatment

TRUNKS AND LIMBS—OTHER PROBLEMS

Symptoms	Kinds of Trees Affected	Probable Trouble	Suggested Treatment
rusty spots or bubbles filled with orange-colored fluid under bark of uppermost branches	white and European white birches	bronze birch borers	**Bark tracing is necessary. Call a tree specialist.**
persistent or intermittent oozing of toxic sap from cracks or other bark injuries; has disagreeable odor	maples, elms, and mulberries	slime flux . . . a disease of the tree's internal wood	**Drill hole at upward angle at base of oozing area and insert a pipe deep enough to permit drainage. Allow to protrude 3–4 inches to prevent oozing' on tree bark. Call a tree specialist.**
swelling, dis-figuration of new growth in April and May; new growth eventu-ally dies	spruce trees	spruce gall aphids	**Spray with a fumi-gant as recom-mended on pages 77–79.**
white, oozy substance on underside of leaves	spruce, poplar, aspen, and cotton-wood trees	cytospora canker (a fungus)	**Feed and water tree. Remove and destroy diseased portions wherever noticeable. Sterilize tools after each tree. Spray with a recommended fungicide, following directions on the label.**

Symptoms	Kinds of Trees Affected	Probable Trouble	Suggested Treatment
knotty growths on branches and twigs	redbud trees	canker (a fungus)	**Prune affected branches during dry weather, and burn them (check local ordinances). Exercise good tree maintenance.**
loosened bark; small tracks on trunk surface beneath bark	elm trees	elm bark beetle (known carrier of Dutch elm disease)	**Spray trunk with Sevin and methoxychlor or Sevin and metacytox.**
tiny holes in trunk and/or limbs	maples, dogwoods, fruits, etc.	borers (may be just under bark or working deeper inside tree)	**Bark tracing required in infested areas. Use borer paste or call tree specialist.**
whitish, silken webs in crotches of trees (tentlike)	wild cherry, chokecherry, other fruit trees, and sometimes deciduous trees	tent caterpillars	**Spray tents and entire tree with malathion. *Never burn tents in tree.***
yellowing and dying twigs	fruit and ornamental trees	twig borer or twig pruner	**Prune off and burn affected twigs, thus destroying the insects and/or eggs.**

FRUIT PROBLEMS

premature fall of fruit; inside of fruit eaten away; punctures in fruit	apple and plum trees	apple or plum curculio (an insect)	**Spray branches at the time blossoms begin to fall. Use stomach poison as recommended on pages 77–79.**

Symptoms	Kinds of Trees Affected	Probable Trouble	Suggested Treatment
maturing fruit falls from tree before ripe; fruit tunneled	apple trees	apple maggots (insect)	Spray branches with stomach poison as recommended on pages 77–79.
blackened fruit	fruit trees	fungus disease	Spray tree with fungicide as recommended on pages 77–79.

MISCELLANEOUS PROBLEMS

Symptoms	Kinds of Trees Affected	Probable Trouble	Suggested Treatment
tap branches sharply over white sheet of paper to see if resulting specks turn to brownish smears when rubbed	evergreens	red spider mites	Spray with miscible oil and ethion in early spring, except on blue spruces. In July, use a fumigant as recommended on pages 77–79.
orange, jelly-like growths (galls) over entire tree	cedars	cedar-apple rust (a fungus)	Spray with a fungicide as recommended on pages 77–79. Pick and burn galls (check local ordinances) in late fall to prevent their development.
generally poor tree growth with signs of decline; dieback of shoot tips (check color of internal wood	maples	wetwood, a disease of the internal wood of the tree	Call a tree specialist. Prune and clean wounds.

Symptoms	Kinds of Trees Affected	Probable Trouble	Suggested Treatment
at various points on trunk by taking test borings—healthy wood almost white; diseased wood is light- to dark-brown and has foul odor; may emit gas or sap)			

Note: If you think your tree is diseased, and cannot identify the problem with certainty, it is best that you consult a tree specialist for expert advice.

THE HOMEOWNER'S GUIDE TO POPULAR TREES

	leaf and fruit	climate and soil preference	characteristics
ASH TREES			
Ash, Black (*Fraxinus nigra*)		States bordering the Great Lakes and Canada, from Pennsylvania to Maine. Moist soils.	Gray, scaly bark.
Ash, Green or Red (*Fraxinus pennsylvania*)		Eastern half of U.S. except for parts of Georgia and Florida. Rich, moist-to-wet soils.	A very hardy tree with gray fissured bark. Gives dense shade. Leaves turn yellow in fall.

	leaf and fruit	climate and soil preference	characteristics
Ash, White *(Fraxinus americana)*		Most portions of eastern half of U.S. Rich, moist soils.	Very popular in the East. Bark is gray. Leaves turn a dull yellow or purple in autumn. Early leaf fall.

BIRCH TREES

	leaf and fruit	climate and soil preference	characteristics
Birch, Canoe (see Birch, Paper)			
Birch, Paper *(Betula papyrifera)*		Parts of northernmost states from Minnesota to Maine inclusive, and all New England. Rich, moist soils.	White, smooth, thin, scaly bark. Pussy Willow— type flower. Yellow leaves in fall. Sometimes called Canoe Birch.
Birch, Red (see Birch, River)			
Birch, River *(Betula nigra)*		Large portions of southeastern U.S. as far west as Kansas. Rich, moist soils.	Used commonly in South as an ornamental tree. Reddish-brown or silver-gray bark with papery scales. Pussy Willow—type flower. Leaves turn a dull yellow in fall. Sometimes called Red Birch.

	leaf and fruit	climate and soil preference	characteristics
Birch, Yellow *(Betula lutea)*		Around Great Lakes region, New England, and in Appalachian Mountains. Rich, well-drained soils.	Bark yellowish to silver-gray; tends to peel. Flowers look like Pussy Willow catkins. Leaves turn reddish-brown in fall. Sweet-smelling leaves and twigs.
ELM TREES Elm, American *(Ulmus americana)*		Eastern half of U.S. Rich, moist soils.	Gray, furrowed bark with scaly ridges. The most stately of all shade trees, but its extinction is threatened by Dutch Elm disease.
Elm, Slippery *(Ulmus rubra)*	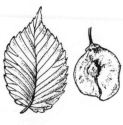	Eastern half of U.S. except in southeasternmost states. Rich, fairly moist soils.	Dark-brown bark. Twigs hairy, rough, and deeply furrowed. Yellow foliage in fall.
Elm, Winged *(Ulmus alata)*		Southeastern states as far west as Texas. Rich, moist soils.	Thin, light-brown bark, irregularly fissured. Yellow foliage in fall.

	leaf and fruit	climate and soil preference	characteristics
Hackberry (*Celtis occidentalis*)		Most of U.S. except for large parts of Southwest and Northwest. Grows well in moist soils but can thrive in poor, sandy soils, too.	Light-brown to gray bark, smooth with corky ridges becoming scaly; fruit is dark cherrylike purple. Wood is soft.
Sugarberry (*Celtis laevigata*)		Southern states from Texas and Kentucky to the Atlantic Coast. Some varieties, however, are found farther north to the Great Lakes area and in the East. Weak, moist soils.	Bark is gray, smooth with corky warts. Bears quarter-inch red, berrylike fruit. Eight varieties of sugarberry grow in the U.S.

EVERGREEN TREES

Cedar, Red (*Juniperus virginiana*)		Eastern half of U.S. except for parts of northern New England, the Dakotas, Minnesota, and southernmost states. Poor, sandy soils.	Reddish-brown bark, blue-green foliage, small purplish berrylike cone, small scalelike needles.

	leaf and fruit	climate and soil preference	characteristics
Fir, Balsam (*Abies balsamea*)	 NEEDLE CONE	Around Great Lakes, in New England, and in parts of Appalachian Mountains. Similar species in parts of western mountains. Rich, moist, well-drained soils.	Popular as the Christmas tree. Flat, rounded-tip needles; purple-brown cones; thin brown or gray bark.
Hemlock, Canadian (*Tsuga canadiens*)	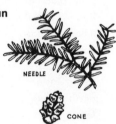 NEEDLE CONE	Parts of northeastern and northwestern corners of U.S. Grows in many different soils but does best in rich, moist soils.	This large forest tree is ideal for hedges and screening. Those growing in Northwest are the largest. Bark is brownish or rust color.
Pine, Austrian (*Pinus nigra*)	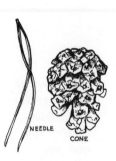 NEEDLE CONE	Most of country, but hardiest in East throughout New England, and the West except the coldest, hottest, and driest locations. Does well in all kinds of soils.	One of the commoner foreign ornamental trees. Tolerant of city dust and smoke. Dense, dark-green foliage; bark is dark gray, fissured into irregular, scaly plates. Stiff dark-green needles come two to a cluster.

	leaf and fruit	climate and soil preference	characteristics
Pine, Lodgepole (*Pinus contorta*)	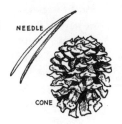	Rocky Mountain and Pacific Coast sections from Canada to southern California. Rich, well-drained soils.	Bark brown, thin, with many loose scales. Needles are two to a cluster, stout, often twisted, yellow-green in color.
Pine, Ponderosa (*Pinus pon- derosa*)	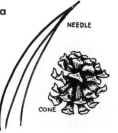	Rocky Mountain and Pacific Coast sections as far east as Colorado. Rich, well-drained soils.	Bark brown or blackish, fur- rowed into ridges; on older trunks becomes yellow-brown. Needles three or two and three in cluster.
Pine, Red (*Pinus resinosa*)	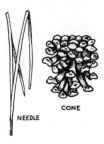	Through Great Lakes region and in north- eastern states. Prefers rich, moist soil but adapts to most soils easily.	A hardy, free- growing tree. Its needles are sharp and stiff, and grow two per cluster. Bark is reddish-brown with flat, scaly plates.
Pine, Scotch (*Pinus sylvestris*)		Hardy through- out the U.S. Thrives on poorer, sandy soils, as well as on better loams.	Bark reddish- brown; on older trunks becoming grayish and fissured into scaly plates. Cones yellow-brown with minute prickles. Resistant to city smoke.

	leaf and fruit	climate and soil preference	characteristics
Pine, Short-Leaf *(Pinus echinata)*	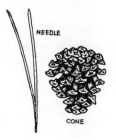 NEEDLE CONE	Most of southeastern U.S. from Maryland to Texas, except for most of Florida. Thrives in sandy soils.	Bark reddishbrown with large, irregular flat scaly plates. Needles grow two or three per cluster.
Pine, Sugar *(Pinus lambertiana)*	NEEDLE 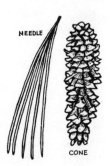 CONE	Parts of Oregon and upper half of California. Rich, welldrained soils.	Bark brown, furrowed into irregular scaly ridges. Needles five in cluster; stout; blue-green in color.
Pine, White *(Pinus strobus)*	 CONE NEEDLE	Parts of Minnesota and Wisconsin, around Great Lakes, New England, and portions of Middle Atlantic States. Adapts to most soils but prefers rich, moist soils.	A hardy tree useful for screening as well as individual plantings. Bark is grayish- to purple-blue with deep cracks. Has five needles per cluster.

	leaf and fruit	climate and soil preference	characteristics
Spruce, Red (*Picea rubens*)		In Great Lakes region from northern Minnesota to New England, and along the Appalachian Mountains. Grows well in all kinds of soils.	Gray-brown scaly bark, short sharp needles. Most common of spruces for ornamental plantings is Colorado Blue Spruce. Other spruces: Engelmann, Sitka, White, Black, and Norway.
Yew (*Taxus*)		Grows throughout the U.S. Rich, well-drained soils.	Bark is reddish-brown and scaly. Has red berries. Generally useful in foundation plantings. Among numerous varieties are Canadian Yew, English Yew, and Japanese Yew.

FRUIT TREES

Apple (*Pyrus malus*)		All climates, but prefers the upper half of U.S. Rich, moist soils.	A hardy tree, but it is important to keep it well pruned and sprayed. Bears fruit in alternate years normally. Some varieties: Delicious Red, Delicious Yellow, Jonathan, Winesap, Cortland.

	leaf and fruit	climate and soil preference	characteristics
Apricot *(Prunus)*		All climates, but prefers upper half of U.S. Rich, dry soils.	A hardy tree, but it is essential to keep it well pruned and sprayed. Bears fruit in alternate years normally. Some varieties: Golden Giant, Hungarian, Sungold, Moorpark.
Cherry, Black *(Prunus serotina)*		Eastern half of U.S. except southern Florida. Rich, well-drained soils.	Reddish-brown to dark-brown bark. Clusters of small white flowers. Other cherry trees include: Tartarian, Napoleon, Montmorency.
Orange *(Citrus)*		Southernmost states from Florida to California. Rich, moist soils.	Requires tropical temperatures to grow. There are many varieties of orange trees, including: Naval, Sour, and Sweet.
Peach *(Prunus)*		Although grown throughout U.S., the preference is around the Great Lakes area. Rich, well-drained soils.	It is important to keep it well pruned and sprayed. Bears fruit in alternate years normally. Some varieties: Albert, Hale Haven, Reliance, Belle of Georgia, J. H. Hale.

	leaf and fruit	climate and soil preference	characteristics
Pear *(Pyrus)*		New England, New York, and westward to the Great Lakes; also in some Pacific Coast areas. Rich, well-drained soils.	This tree is subject to borer attacks and pear blight (a fungus). Bears fruit in alternate years normally. Some varieties: Bartlett, Seckel, Clapp's, and Favorite.
Pecan *(Carya illinoensis)*		Mississippi Valley region and Southwest. Rich, moist soils.	Light-brown or gray bark deeply furrowed and cracked. 1"- to 2"-long nuts are edible. Useful as an ornamental or crop tree.
Plum *(Prunus)*		Although grown throughout U.S., the preference is the Great Lakes region. Rich to poor, moist soils.	Bears fruit on alternate years normally. Some varieties: Stanley, Burbank, and Damson.
Quince *(Cydonia vulgaris)*		Most of Eastern half of U.S. Moist but well-drained soils.	The branches of this tree usually grow crooked and distorted. Subject to borer attacks.

	leaf and fruit	climate and soil preference	characteristics
Walnut, Black *(Juglans nigra)*		Eastern half of U.S. except New England, Florida, along Gulf Coast, and parts of Wisconsin and Minnesota. Rich, well-drained soils.	Dark-brown, thick bark. Hardwood. Commonly used as a shade tree. When planting, allow plenty of space to grow; avoid placing too close to house.
MAGNOLIA TREES Magnolia, Cucumber Tree *(Magnolia acuminata)*		Most parts of eastern and southeastern states, except along Atlantic Coast. Rich, moist soils.	Light-brown, scaly bark; bell-shaped flower. Fruit resembles a cucumber.
Magnolia, Southern *(Magnolia grandiflora)*		Prefers most parts of the southeastern states but grows throughout the U.S. Rich, moist soils.	Thick, light-gray to light-brown bark. Large, cup-shaped flower gives off strong, pleasant odor.
Poplar, Yellow (Tulip Tree) *(Liriodendron tulipifera)*		Eastern third of U.S. except southern Florida and parts of New England. Rich, moist soil.	Tallest of eastern hardwood trees. Common as an ornamental tree. Thick, brown furrowed bark. Green-yellow, tulip-shaped flower. Gives yellow foliage in fall.

	leaf and fruit	climate and soil preference	characteristics
Sweet Bay (Magnolia virginiana)		Grows along Atlantic Coast from southern New England to Key West, Florida; also along Gulf Coast to Texas. Rich, moist soils.	Gray or light-brown bark. Small cup-shaped flower. Almost like an evergreen in southernmost states.

MAPLE TREES

Box Elder (Acer negundo)		Most of eastern half of U.S. except for New England, New York, and parts of Pennsylvania and Florida. Rich to fair, well-drained soils.	Thin, grayish-brown bark irregularly fissured.
Maple, Big Leaf (see Maple, Sugar)			
Maple, Black (Acer nigrum)		Northeastern quarter of U.S. except northern New England. Good quality, well-drained soil.	Furrowed bark with irregular ridges, often very coarse toward base of trunk. A hardwood. Leaves turn yellow in autumn.

	leaf and fruit	climate and soil preference	characteristics
Maple, Norway (Acer plata- noides)		Prefers eastern U.S. and the Pacific and Rocky Mountain areas, although widely trans- planted. Rich, well-drained soil.	Popular for land- scaping. Highly resistant to insect pests, smoke and dirt, it is a good city tree. Dark-gray bark. Leaf similar but broader than leaf of Sugar Maple. Foliage turns yellow in the fall. Schwedler's Maple is the red-leaf variety.
Maple, Red (Acer rubrum)		Most of eastern third of U.S. from western end of Great Lakes to eastern Texas. Moist to wet soils.	Smooth gray bark, reddish twigs. Foliage turns crimson and wine red in autumn. A good shade tree.
Maple, Schwedler's (see Maple, Norway)			
Maple, Silver or Swamp (Acer saccharinum)		Eastern half of U.S. except for extreme north- ern and south- ern parts. Wet soil.	Light-gray, smooth bark. A softwood. Also known as Soft Maple.

	leaf and fruit	climate and soil preference	characteristics
Maple, Sugar (*Acer saccharum*)		Eastern half of U.S. except for southeastern-most states. (Big-Leaf Maple is similar, and grows along Pacific Coast.) Good quality, well-drained soil.	A popular shade tree sometimes called Rock Maple. Furrowed bark with irregular ridges often very coarse toward base of trunk. Leaves turn yellow, orange, or red in fall.

OAK TREES

Oak, Black (Rock) (*Quercus velutina*)		Eastern half of U.S. except extreme northern and southern portions. Adapts easily to most soil conditions.	Brownish, thick bark with ridges. Inner bark is yellow or orange, an important characteristic in identifying it. Leaves turn red-tan to brown in fall. Sometimes called Yellow Oak.
Oak, Blackjack (*Quercus marilandica*)		Southeastern quarter of U.S. except some Gulf Coast areas and Florida. Well-drained, sandy soils.	A small tree with blackish, thick, rough bark. Leaves turn brown and yellow in fall.

	leaf and fruit	climate and soil preference	characteristics
Oak, Bur (*Quercus macrocarpa*)		Eastern half of U.S. except for parts of New England, states along the Atlantic Coast and Gulf of Mexico. Prefers moist soils but will adapt to dry, sandy soils.	Gray-brown bark with deep furrows. Scaly, hairylike acorn.
Oak, Chestnut (*Quercus montana*)		Mainly in Appalachian Mountains and in most Middle Atlantic States. Grows in dry, poor soils.	A hardwood tree normally found growing on the sides of hills. Dark-brown bark. Leaves turn orange in fall.
Oak, Northern Red (*Quercus borealis*)		Eastern half of U.S. except for large parts of southernmost states. Rich, well-drained soils.	One of the largest oaks. Ideal for shade. A hardwood. Bark is dark brown. Leaves turn red in fall.
Oak, Pin (*Quercus palustris*)		Prefers Middle Atlantic and midwestern states, but transplanted widely across the U.S. Moist soils.	A popular tree in landscaping because of its fast rate of growth compared to other oaks. Grayish-brown bark, fissured and scaly in texture. Gives brilliant fall colors.

	leaf and fruit	climate and soil preference	characteristics
Oak, Post *(Quercus stellata)*		Parts of Middle Atlantic States and southeastern quarter of U.S., except some Gulf Coast areas and southern Florida. Good to poor, dry to moist soils.	Grayish bark with broad, scaly ridges.
Oak, Scarlet *(Quercus coccinea)*		Eastern third of U.S., except for most of New England, all of Florida, and parts of southern states adjacent to Florida. Dry, sandy soils.	Strongly resembles the Pin Oak in leaf and structure, but has larger leaf. Leaves turn a brilliant red in fall. Wood is reddish-brown. Dark or grayish bark with scaly ridges.
Oak, Southern Red *(Quercus falcata)*		Most of southeastern U.S. except southern Florida. Rich, dry, sandy soils.	A popular shade and ornamental tree in southeastern states. Bark is gray to reddish dark brown and fissured into narrow ridges. Leaves are brown and orange in fall. Also known as Swamp Red Oak and Spanish Oak.

	leaf and fruit	climate and soil preference	characteristics
Oak, Swamp Chestnut (*Quercus prinus*)		Most portions of southeastern quarter of U.S. Rich, moist soils.	Usually found in swampy areas. Brownish-gray bark, ridged and scaly.
Oak, Swamp White (*Quercus bicolor*)		Northeastern quarter of U.S. except extreme northern areas. Rich, moist-to-wet soils.	Usually found in swampy areas. Grayish ridged and scaly bark. Closely related to the Swamp Chestnut Oak of the South.
Oak, Water (*Quercus nigra*)		Most portions of southeastern states. Prefers rich, wet soils but can adapt to dryer soils.	In its earliest growth years its bark is dark gray and smooth; later it breaks up into irregular ridges. Leaves turn yellow in fall.
Oak, White (*Quercus alba*)		Most of eastern half of U.S. except for extreme northern and southern points. Rich, well-drained soils.	A popular tree in New England. Bark is light-gray and scaly in texture. Leaves are purple-red to pink in spring and fall.

	leaf and fruit	climate and soil preference	characteristics
Oak, Willow (*Quercus phellos*)		Most of southeastern states. Rich, moist soils.	A popular shade tree in the South. Wood is a reddish-brown color. Long, willow-like leaves.
Oak, Yellow (*see* Oak, Black)			

WILLOW TREES

	leaf and fruit	climate and soil preference	characteristics
Aspen, Bigtooth (*Populus grandidentata*)		Most parts of northeastern quarter of U.S. Rich, moist soil.	Smooth greenish bark becomes dark brown with age. A soft wood. A fast grower in burned-out or eroded areas.
Basswood, American (Linden) (*Tilia americana*)		Most of northeastern quarter of U.S. Rich, well-drained soils.	Gray furrowed bark. Fruit seeds resemble a praying mantis. Flowers give off scent in late spring.

	leaf and fruit	climate and soil preference	characteristics
Cottonwood, Eastern *(Populus deltoides)*		Most parts of eastern half of U.S. (Other cottonwoods in northern plain areas and Northwest.) Adapts to a variety of moist soils.	A common shade tree, especially on prairies. Bark is yellowish in color.
Poplar, Balsam *(Populus taca-mahaca)*		States bordering Canada, from Minnesota to Maine. Moist, sandy soils.	Reddish-brown smooth bark becomes gray and furrowed. Catkin-like flower seed.
Willow, Black *(Salix nigra)*		Eastern half of U.S., including parts of Texas and neighboring states. Exceptions: southern Florida and northern Maine. Rich, wet soil.	Dark-brown or blackish bark with scaly ridges. Sometimes called Swamp Willow.

Willow, Swamp
   (*see* Willow, Black)

	leaf and fruit	climate and soil preference	characteristics
Willow, Weeping *(Salix baby-lonica)*		Almost all parts of U.S. Rich to poor wet soils.	A fast-growing tree that is smoke- and smog-resistant. Can grow from twig cuttings implanted in wet ground. A native of China, this tree is now transplanted throughout world. Caution: this tree spreads its roots widely, and care should be exercised when planting in drainpipe and septic-system areas.
OTHER TREES Ailanthus *(Ailanthus altissima)*		Transplanted throughout U.S. Almost any moist soils, even poor-quality soils.	Smooth gray-brown bark with cracks. Resistant to dirt, smoke, carbon dioxide, and insects.
Beech, American *(Fagus grandifolia)*		Eastern third of U.S. except for most of Florida. Rich soil with good drainage.	A large, stately tree with hard reddish wood and bluish-gray thin smooth bark. Leaves turn a golden bronze in fall. Among other beech varieties: the Copper Beech and Weeping Beech.

	leaf and fruit	climate and soil preference	characteristics
Bitternut (*Carya cordiformis*)		Eastern half of U.S. except for northern Minnesota, Wisconsin, and Maine, and along the Atlantic and Gulf coasts from the Carolinas to Louisiana. Rich, wet soils.	Grayish-brown, scaly bark. Bright yellow buds. Sometimes called Swamp Hickory.
Black Gum (*see* Tupelo, Black)			
Buttonball (*see* Sycamore, American)			
Catalpa, Northern (*Catalpa speciosa*)		Widely transplanted throughout U.S. Adaptable to many moist soil conditions.	Reddish-brown bark with scaly ridges. Useful in cities and along roadways.
Chestnut (*Castanea dentata*)		Appalachian Mountains and Ohio Valley areas. Rich, well-drained soils.	Dark-brown bark. Although extinction of this once popular tree is threatened by a chestnut blight, efforts are still being made to save it.

	leaf and fruit	climate and soil preference	characteristics
Dogwood (Cornus florida)	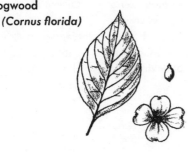	Throughout most of U.S. except for parts of Texas and neighboring states (Flowering Dogwood in Middle Atlantic and southeastern states; Pacific Dogwood on West Coast). Rich, well-drained soil.	There are 17 species of dogwood in U.S. Others include: Chinese Dogwood and Cornelian Cherry. Probably the most popular of flowering trees used for landscaping. Bark, divided into small squares in lower trunk areas, is reddish-brown to gray. Small red berries and colorful foliage in fall. White or red flowers in spring.
Ginkgo (Ginkgo biloba)		Widely cultivated and transplanted throughout U.S. Moist good to poor soils.	Native of China. Disease- and insect-resistant. Golden yellow leaves in fall.
Greenwattle Acacia (Acacia decurrens)		Along Pacific Coast from California to Texas. Adapts to a wide range of soil conditions.	Native of Australia. Extensively planted on the West Coast. Gives yellow flowers.

	leaf and fruit	climate and soil preference	characteristics
Hawthorn (Crataegus)		Virtually all of U.S. except parts of Southwest. Good to poor dry soils.	Over 800 species of this tree (examples: Ashe, English, Little Hip, Cockspur, Scarlet Haw). Long, profuse, toothy, and irregular thorns. Flowers are white, and grow in small clusters.
Hickory, Shagbark (Carya ovata)		Most of eastern U.S. except for parts of northern New England, Florida, and Gulf Coast. Rich, moist soils.	Gray, furrowed bark that's loose. Leaves turn yellow to brown in fall.
Hickory, Swamp (see Bitternut)			
Holly, American (Ilex opaca)		Most of southeastern quarter of U.S. but widely transplanted throughout country. Adaptable to different soils, but prefers moist soils.	Protect this tree when it is newly planted to prevent exposure of buds to winter cold. Other species of Holly Tree found in eastern U.S.

	leaf and fruit	climate and soil preference	characteristics
Holly, English *(Ilex aquifolium)*		Successfully planted throughout the U.S. Sandy, well-drained soils.	A handsome, hardy tree with red berries and sharp prickly leaves. Branches useful in Christmas decorations. A native of western and southern Europe.
Horse Chestnut *(Aesculus hippocastanum)*		Widely transplanted throughout the U.S. Rich, well-drained soils.	Bark is brownish, thin, fissured, and scaly. Quick to adapt when transplanted. Native of the Balkans. Large, showy flowers sometimes spotted with red dots.
Judas Tree *(see Redbud)*			
Larch (Tamarack) *(Larix laricina)*		States surrounding the Great Lakes, and all New England. Rich, wet soils.	Bark reddish-brown and scaly. Needles many in clusters on short spur branches.
Linden (see Basswood, American, in section "Willow Trees")			

	leaf and fruit	climate and soil preference	characteristics
Locust, Black (*Robinia pseudoacacia*)		Originated in Middle Atlantic States but has been widely transplanted and spread by natural propagation throughout eastern half of U.S. Adapts easily to different soils, from good to poor and wet to dry.	Brown to gray bark, thick, rough, and furrowed. Drought-resistant, but menaced by borers and fungus. Short thorns at base of each leaf.
Locust, Honey (*Gleditsia triacanthos*)		Large portions of Midwest below Great Lakes region downward to the Gulf of Mexico, but transplanted widely. Prefers rich, well-drained soils.	A large tree that is fast becoming popular as a shade tree and a replacement for the American Elm. Sometimes called Thorny Locust. Dark-gray or blackish bark. Thorns along trunk and twigs. Drought-resistant. Moraine Locust is the thornless variety, also popular among home-owners.
Locust, Thorny (*see* **Locust, Honey**)			

	leaf and fruit	climate and soil preference	characteristics
Mimosa (or Silk Tree) *(Mimosa albizia)*		Mostly southern states across the country, but transplanted widely. Sandy, moist soils preferred, but is adaptable to other conditions.	Ideal as an ornamental tree. Pink or white flowers, depending on variety.
Mountain Ash *(Sorbus americana)*		Rocky Mountain area from Canada to Texas; also Great Lakes region from Pennsylvania to Maine. Sandy, dry soils.	Transplanted widely as an ornamental tree. Smooth, gray bark. Showy clusters of berries.
Mulberry, Red *(Morus rubra)*		Eastern half of U.S. except for northern portions of the Great Lakes region and most of New England. Adapts to most soils from rich to poor and moist to dry.	Dark-brown scaly bark, toothy leaf. Often subject to bleeding cankers.

	leaf and fruit	climate and soil preference	characteristics
Palm, Washington *(Washingtonia filitera)*	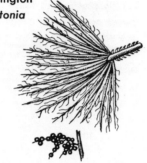	Very restricted to natural habitat, although widely planted. Grows in deserts, particularly near water holes. Found mainly in western U.S. Moist, sandy soils.	Largest of our native palm trees. Fan-shaped leaves, measuring 4'–5' across.
Palmetto, Cabbage *(Sabal palmetto)*		Grows along South Atlantic and Gulf coasts, but transplanted widely on West Coast. Moist, sandy soils.	Fan-shaped leaves 4'–7' long. Edible buds or cabbages. Useful as an ornamental tree.
Pepperidge (see Tupelo, Black)			
Persimmon, Common *(Diospyros virginiana)*		Southeastern U.S., including the Mississippi Valley. Rich, well-drained soils.	Dark-brown, thick bark. White flower. Edible fruit.
Plane, American (see Sycamore, American)			

	leaf and fruit	climate and soil preference	characteristics
Redbud, Eastern or American (Cercis canadensis)		Eastern half of U.S. except near coasts along Atlantic and Gulf and all New England. Rich, moist soils.	Deep-brown bark, smooth on young trees and furrowed on older trees. Favored as an ornamental tree. Pink to purple blossoms in March or April. This tree is also commonly known as the Judas Tree.
Sassafras (Sassafras albidum)		Eastern half of U.S. except parts of Minnesota, Wisconsin, northern New England, and southern Florida. Dry or well-drained acid soils.	Reddish-brown, furrowed bark. Leaves grow in three different shapes, resembling fork, glove, and spoon. Small yellow-green blossoms give a lacy effect in spring. Orange to scarlet colors in fall. Aromatic twigs.

Serviceberry
(see Shadbush)

	leaf and fruit	climate and soil preference	characteristics
Shadbush (Service-berry) *(Amelanchier canadensis)*		Most of U.S. except Texas and neighboring states to the north, along Gulf and South Atlantic coasts, and parts of California. Does well in poor, rich, dry, or damp soils.	Some 20 species of this tree grow in this country. Grayish-brown, smooth bark. White blossoms in spring.
Silk Tree (*see* Mimosa)			
Sour Gum (*see* Tupelo, Black)			
Sweet Gum *(Liquidambar styraciflua)*		Large parts of the southeastern states, but has been transplanted widely throughout U.S. Rich, moist soils.	Thick gray furrowed bark; thick reddish-brown twigs, often with corky ridges. Normally insect- and disease-free. Not suitable in places where temperature drops below zero. Leaves turn brilliant wine red, gold, and purple in fall.

	leaf and fruit	climate and soil preference	characteristics
Sycamore, American (Plane) *(Platanus occidentalis)*		Eastern half of U.S. except portions of Minnesota, Wisconsin, and northern New England. Similar species grow in parts of California and Arizona. Adapts to varieties of soils, dry to wet and rich to poor.	Thin white or yellowish scaly bark with brown patches. Bark peels off in sheets. Leaves fall from midsummer to Christmas. Commonly called Buttonball Tree. A good city tree.

Tamarack
  (see Larch)

Tulip Tree (see Poplar, Yellow, in section "Magnolia Trees")

	leaf and fruit	climate and soil preference	characteristics
Tupelo, Black *(Nyssa sylvatica)*		Most of eastern third of U.S. and parts of Mississippi Valley except northern New England and southern Florida. Rich, moist soils.	Reddish-brown bark with irregular and block-shaped ridges. Called Black Gum, Sour Gum, and Pepperidge. Smooth, shiny leaves becoming bright red in autumn.
Yellowwood, American *(Cladrastis lutea)*		Grows in southeastern states and also from New England southward along Atlantic Coast. Rich, moist, well-drained soils.	Short trunk, smooth gray-brown bark. Should be transplanted in early spring. Resistant to fungus and drought.

SELECTED BIBLIOGRAPHY

Burks, Bernard D., "Insects, Enemies of Insects," Yearbook Separate No. 2344,
  Yearbook of Agriculture, United States Department of Agriculture, Washington,
  D.C., 1952.
Garver, Harry L., *Lightning Protection for the Farm,* Farmers' Bulletin No. 2136,
  United States Department of Agriculture, Washington, D.C., 1963.
Miller, H. C., and Silverborg, S. B., *Maple Tree Problems,* State University College
  of Forestry, Syracuse University, Syracuse, N.Y., 1958.
Thompson, A. Robert, *Tree Bracing,* Tree Preservation Bulletin No. 3, United
  States Department of the Interior, Washington, D.C., 1959.
The Japanese Beetle: How to Control It, Farmers' Bulletin No. 2151, United States
  Department of Agriculture, Washington, D.C., 1962.
Know Your Soil, Agriculture Information Bulletin No. 267, Soil Conservation Ser-
  vice, United States Department of Agriculture, Washington, D.C., 1963.
Mantids, Corres. Aid No. 1, United States Department of Agriculture, Entomol-
  ogy Research Branch, Washington, D.C., February, 1955.
Maple Diseases and Their Control, Home & Garden Bulletin No. 81, United States
  Department of Agriculture, Washington, D.C., 1962.
*1980 Cornell Recommendations for Pest Control for Commercial Production and Maintenance
  of Trees and Shrubs,* N.Y. State College of Agriculture & Life Sciences, a statu-
  tory college of the State University, at Cornell University.
Pruning Shade Trees and Repairing Their Injuries, Home & Garden Bulletin No. 83,
  United States Department of Agriculture, Washington, D.C., 1962.
Trees—Yearbook of Agriculture, United States Department of Agriculture, Washington, D.C., 1949.

INDEX

stumps, tree, 28, 36
subsoil, 37
sucker growth, 62, 65
sugar, 11
sugar maple trees, 77, 86
sugars, manufacture of, 37, 50
sulfur, 38
summer, 14, 18, 23, 35, 56, 65, 67, 70, 75, 83, 86, 104
sunlight, 11, 13, 14, 23, 25, 32, 34, 45, 47, 53, 55, 56, 69
sunscald, 29, 30, 32, 33, 58, 65, 73
support, artificial tree, 30, 32, 35, 88, 90, 100
sweet soil, 38
swimming pool, 20
sycamore trees, 16, 97
syrups, 11

Tanglefoot, 84
tar spot, 75
temperature, 83
10,000 Garden Questions, 45
tender-barked trees, 65
tent caterpillar, 75
tents, caterpillar, 75, 80, 84, 86
termites, 74, 85
thimbles, 92, 93, 95
thin-barked trees, 32, 63, 64, 84, 86
tile vents, 91
timber, 11
tools, 61, 71, 72, 87, 101, 102; *see also* individual tools
tools, pruning, 87
tools, sterilization of, 61, 87
topcut, 61, 62
top-heavy trees, 14
topography, 83
topsoil, 31, 37, 53, 100
transplanting, 28, 31, 34, 59, 92, 94
tree experts, professional, 12, 15, 16, 27, 48, 57, 62, 63, 71, 77, 79, 84, 102–5
Tree Experts Manual, 16
tree identification, 20, 126–54
tree-planting programs, 17
trees
  benefits of, 9, 10, 11, 17, 18, 21, 22, 29
  components of, 13
  cutting down, 26–27
  functional uses around home, 17, 18, 24–26
  growth, rate of, *see* Chart C, 110
  healing powers of, 12, 14, 65
  large, 52, 98
  life expectancy of, 16
  mysteries about, 12
  newly planted, 32
  nursery-grown trees, *see* Chart A, 106
  problems with, 16
  resistance to hazards, 16, 37, 38, 47, 50, 54
  selecting, 26, 28
  size at maturity, *see* Chart B, 108
  small, 42, 52, 53, 54, 59, 79, 83
  tall, 97
  that interfere, 19, 20, 21, 22, 23

trunk, tree, 13, 27, 33, 34, 48, 50, 51, 60, 63, 67, 68, 74, 75, 76, 84–86, 88, 90, 91, 94, 97, 100, 105
trunk injection, 57
tubes, copper, 98
tulip trees, 16
turpentine, 11
twigs, 26, 36, 43, 47, 56, 59, 63, 71, 76, 77; *see also* branches

Unasylva, 10
undercut, 61, 62
Underwriters Laboratories, Inc., 98
University of California, 81
utility lines, 19, 27, 59, 72, 101, 105

vacuum-cleaner dust, 42
vegetable remains, 41, 51
ventilation, 37
vents, tile, 91
vermiculite, 50
vines, 69
vista work, 59, 69

Wallace, Dr. George J., 81
walnut trees, 86
water, 10, 14, 32, 36
  as a tree need, 11, 13, 38, 47, 48, 53, 54, 55, 58, 73
  drinking, 10
  for compost heap, 44
  for planting trees, 31
  in drainage, 42, 66, 90
  in liquid fertilizer, 51
  in oil spray, 86
  pressure in heartwood, 68
water lines, 19, 21, 22, 23, 34
water supplies, 10
water table, 19
watering, 29, 33, 53, 54, 85
watershed areas, 10
waxlike substance, 84
weather, 10, 44, 83, 85
weed killer, 86
weeds, 42, 43
welling, tree, 88, 89, 100
western grebe, 81
Whitehead, Stanley B., 41
wild-growing trees, 34
willow trees, 17, 26, 34, 65
wilt, 83
wind, 9, 10, 18, 24, 26, 32, 33, 36, 58, 76, 80, 87, 90, 105
windbreaks, 18, 23, 54
winter, 12, 18, 23, 26, 29, 30, 33, 53, 54, 67, 70
wire, 67, 101
wood, 11, 76, 85
wood chips, 56
wood screw, 93, 94, 96
woodland, 28, 36
wounds, 67

yew trees, 16
young trees, 32, 53, 58, 66, 68

zinc, 11, 38